Farewell to God

Farewell to God

My Reasons for Rejecting the Christian Faith

Charles Templeton

McCLELLAND & STEWART

Cloth edition published 1996
Trade paperback edition 1999

LIBRARY AND ARCHIVES CANADA CATALOGUING IN PUBLICATION

Templeton, Charles, 1915-
    Farewell to God: my reasons for rejecting the Christian faith

ISBN: 978-0-7710-8508-6
ISBN: 978-0-7710-8422-5 (bound)

1. Christianity – Controversial literature. I. Title.

BL2747.T44 1999   230   C96-930669-5

We acknowledge the financial support of the Government of Canada through the Book Publishing Industry Development Program and that of the Government of Ontario through the Ontario Media Development Corporation's Ontario Book Initiative. We further acknowledge the support of the Canada Council for the Arts and the Ontario Arts Council for our publishing program.

Typesetting by M&S, Toronto
Printed and bound in Canada

McClelland & Stewart
75 Sherbourne Street
Toronto, Ontario
M5A 2P9
www.mcclelland.com

4 5 6   10 09 08 07

Contents

Author's Note

Permit me to make it clear that this book is not the product of any bias or nurtured grievance against the Christian church, its clergy, or its members. Almost without exception they have been kind and charitable to me – and this despite my public renunciation of my Christian faith and my rejection of the beliefs on which the Christian religion is based.

Am I critical of the church because it did not give me a hearing or deal with me in kindness and charity? The opposite has been so. I oppose the Christian church because, for all the good it sometimes does, it presumes to speak in the name of God and to propound and advocate beliefs that are outdated, demonstrably untrue, and often, in their various manifestations, deleterious to individuals and to society.

NOTE: For the most part, quotations from the New Testament are from the New Revised Standard version of the Holy Bible; quotations from the Old Testament are from the King James version.

For Madeleine

Farewell to God

A Personal Word

*I*n 1936 my life took a sudden, unexpected, and profound change in direction – a change that radically altered the next twenty-one years of my life. I became what is commonly called a "born-again Christian."

Our family consisted of five children and our mother. Father had left us some three years earlier to take a temporary job in Montreal at Henry Morgan & Company. That having not worked out, he had moved sequentially to Winnipeg, Edmonton, and Vancouver. We heard from him through an occasional letter, but otherwise, in effect, he was gone.

With little or no money coming into the household, we had no choice but to go "on relief," as it was then called, and supplement that social assistance by renting out the bedrooms in the house in which we lived. The next few years were spent with strangers in the hall and on the stairs, seething resentment and aching kidneys over their extended occupancy of the one bathroom, and the worrisome sight of Mother growing increasingly wan and dispirited from work and worry.

As winter descended, I sifted through the furnace ashes each morning for any unconsumed nuggets of coal, and scoured the neighbourhood for blocks around looking for broken tree branches or discarded wood of any kind. Stews were made substantial with flour and barley and we filled up on two-day-old bread (it was cheaper) and one of two standard desserts: bread pudding or "fish-eye" (tapioca) pudding.

It seemed the cheque from the government was always late, some-times by as much as a week. There was one unforgettable twenty-four-hour period when there was nothing – not a morsel of food – in the house to eat. How often the six of us poised hushed and motion-less, like animals freezing when a predator is near, until the bill-collector had gone from the front door. I can still see Mother at the kitchen table counting the coins kept in a china teapot, dabbing at her eyes with a handkerchief . . .

AND THEN, THE FAMILY "got religion."

I had just found a job as sports cartoonist for the Toronto *Globe*. I had made a drawing of the Toronto Maple Leafs' Kid Line – Primeau, Jackson, and Conacher – and had taken the drawing to Mike Rodden, the sports editor. Without any comment, he assigned me to do a sketch of the famed Australian sculler, Bobby Pearce, who was scheduled to race the following day at the Canadian National Exhibition. He liked it and hired me. My weekly salary in dollars matched my age in years – eighteen.

ONE NIGHT SOME WEEKS later, I returned home at 3:00 a.m. heavy with depression. Having completed my duties at the newspa-per, I had gone with a colleague in the sports department to a private strip show in a house in the east end of the city. It was a sleazy affair. The women lacked grace and assumed an air of boredom. As they stripped in the unflattering light, some revealed stretch marks, surgi-cal scars, and marbled cellulite.

There was a mirror in the entrance hall to our home, and I stopped before it, remaining for perhaps a minute. I didn't like the man I saw there. I went softly down the hall to my bedroom, not wanting to dis-turb Mother, but she was awake, waiting for me, her so-called "man of the house." I sat on the side of her bed. She began to talk to me about God, and about how she longed to see me with the other chil-dren in church.

I heard little of what she was saying; my mind was doing an inven-tory of my life. I felt shoddy, unclean. I am at a loss to understand what I did next. A number of facile explanations present themselves:

that I yearned for a satisfactory father figure; that I wanted somehow to repay my mother for her years of loneliness and struggle by accepting her new-found faith; that my early adolescent experiments at sex, innocent enough in retrospect, filled me with guilt. Whatever the reasons, I said, "Mom, I'm going to my room."

As I went down the hall, I was forming the first fumbling words of a prayer in my mind. I knelt by my bed in the darkness. Suddenly, it was as though a black blanket had been draped over me. A sense of guilt pervaded my entire mind and body. The only words that would come were, "Lord, come down. Come down . . ."

I found myself – I don't know how much later – my head in my hands, crouched small on the floor at the centre of a vast, dark emptiness. Slowly, a weight began to lift, a weight as heavy as I. It passed through my thighs, my torso, my arms and shoulders, and lifted off. An ineffable warmth began to suffuse my body. It seemed that a light had turned on in my chest and that it had cleansed me. I felt, in the biblical phrase, that I could have leaped over a wall.

I hardly dared breathe, fearing that I might alter or end the moment. And I heard myself whispering softly over and over again, "Thank you, Lord. Thank you. Thank you. Thank you."

Later, in bed, I lay quietly at the centre of a radiant, overwhelming, all-pervasive happiness. Outside my window dawn was suffusing the sky and some birds had begun their first tentative twittering. As I lay there I began to laugh, softly, out of an indescribable sense of well-being at the centre of all-encompassing joy.

THE EXPERIENCE dramatically changed the direction of my life.

With astonishing ingenuousness I related what had happened to some of my associates in the sports department at the *Globe*. At first there were looks of frowning incredulity in their faces. These gave way to off-colour kidding. As the days passed, all the preacher-and-the-choir-girl jokes were dusted off. Raunchiness reached for new heights. It was all good-natured male badinage, but it soon became evident that I had distanced myself from them and that we were no longer quite at ease with one another. And when the time came some months later to notify Tommy Munns, the assistant sports editor, that

I was leaving the paper to prepare for the ministry, he smiled his off-centre grin and said, "Good luck, Templeton. I think you're nuts, but good luck."

BILLY GRAHAM AND I sensed an immediate affinity when we met, and it led to a close and continuing friendship that has been sustained – albeit now only occasionally – over fifty years.

Billy and I met in the spring of 1945, backstage at a Youth for Christ rally at a jam-packed Chicago Stadium. We were in our twenties. As he was being introduced to preach, he leaned toward me and whispered, "Pray for me, Chuck, I'm scared to death."

I returned to Toronto and began to organize my own Saturday-night youth rallies. Within weeks some sixteen hundred young people gathered every Saturday night in Toronto's Massey Hall.

Youth for Christ was a North American phenomenon in the 1940s. The atmosphere was informal and upbeat – more like show business than church – and young people flocked to the meetings in their thousands in various American cities. Toronto Youth for Christ, in a refurbished and expanded Massey Hall, was the largest, with a weekly attendance of approximately twenty-five hundred.

When a few months later a group of us formed Youth for Christ International, I was named one of three vice-presidents and, at our first meeting, moved that we appoint Graham our evangelist-at-large. A team was selected to carry the Youth for Christ emphasis to Europe. Torrey Johnston, a young Chicago minister, was the nominal leader of the group, a robust baritone by the name of Stratton Shufeld would supply the music, and Billy and I would alternate in the pulpit.

The movement had grown like a prairie wildfire and was attracting worldwide attention. When the four of us departed the Chicago airport for London, a noisy throng of hundreds of teenagers saw us off. William Randolph Hearst, the owner of the Hearst newspaper chain, assigned a reporter and a photographer to travel with us and instructed all his newspapers to devote daily coverage to our activities. A *Life* magazine photographer and reporter dogged our every step as we prepared to leave. *Time*, *Newsweek*, and all the wire services provided coverage.

Nightly, over a period of three weeks, we held mass youth rallies in the British Isles and Western Europe. No building was large enough to house the youngsters who flocked to the meetings.

BACK IN CANADA my days were filled with activity. The church I had founded in Toronto three years earlier – with a membership comprising my mother, my brothers and sisters, and a few friends – functioned in an attractive, white-limestone church building on Toronto's Avenue Road, abandoned when the United Church of Canada was formed. I had rented it, personally paying for it with an advance of $600 for six months. I ran an advertisement on the church page in the newspapers and opened the doors. The church seated twelve hundred. On the first Sunday morning there were twelve people present. The evening-service attendance was just short of a hundred. Within six months people were being turned away from the Sunday-evening service and again at a 9:00 p.m. service especially designed for young people. After two years we added a balcony on three sides to accommodate the crowds and put the overflow in the basement and an adjoining wing. On the eve of the formal dedication of the remodelled sanctuary, the building was gutted by fire, the blaze kindled by a sixteen-year-old boy, a member of the choir. We never did learn why.

But the congregation would not be deterred, and the people of Toronto – many belonging to other churches – contributed to the rebuilding. During this time, services were held in the nearby Masonic Temple on Yonge Street. When the enlarged church was reopened, we turned away hundreds every Sunday evening.

And so things continued for seven years.

BUT ALL WAS NOT well. I was facing a growing dilemma. Increasingly, I was beginning to question some of the essentials of the Christian faith. I had gone through a conversion experience as an incredibly green youth of nineteen and, with only a grade-nine education, I lacked the intellectual skills and the theological training needed to buttress my beliefs when – as was inevitable – questions and doubts began to plague me. I wanted very much to believe. At first I accepted the beliefs of the people I fell in with after my conversion experience, but now that was not enough. I read widely in every spare minute: on trains and planes, in bed before sleep. Slowly, and much against my will for I could perceive the jeopardy in it, my reason had begun to challenge and sometimes to rebut the central beliefs of the Christian faith.

I had always doubted the Genesis account of creation and could never accept the monstrous evil of an endless hell, but now other doubts were surfacing and, having no one to discuss them with, my personal devotions began to flag.

Finally after countless hours of inner struggle and frequent bouts of despair, I decided that, if I were to continue in the ministry and grow with the years, I would have to undertake formal training. At the suggestion of Dr. James Mutchmor, head of the Department of Evangelism and Social Services of the United Church of Canada, I applied to Princeton Theological Seminary in Princeton, New Jersey. Back came a letter from the dean pointing out that the seminary was a graduate school and that among the requirements for admission was a B.A. from an accredited university. He added that, if I completed high school and earned a B.A., he would be happy to consider my application.

I wrote him, pressing for an opportunity to present my case. A date was agreed upon. By a remarkable coincidence, the guest speaker at the chapel on the morning of my appointment was Dr. George Pidgeon, moderator of the United Church of Canada. After the service, Dr. John Mackay, the president of the seminary, mentioned to him that a man from Toronto named Templeton, seeking to be admitted as a special student, was coming to see him. Pidgeon expressed surprise but said, "I know Templeton's work in Toronto. If he wants to return to study, do what you can to help him."

Much to my delight – and after a grilling on my theological views – I was informed that I would be admitted as a "special student." I was also told that, although I would be required to complete the three years' work for a Bachelor of Theology degree and write all the examinations, I would not be granted the degree as I did not have the prerequisites.

I returned to Toronto and notified the Avenue Road Church

congregation that I was leaving. It was a sad and sometimes tearful time and there were moments when I wavered in indecision. But the die had been cast.

EARLY THAT SUMMER, I flew to Montreat, North Carolina, to spend a day with Billy and Ruth Graham. Billy and I had become close friends, although our backgrounds were radically different. Billy was a country boy, raised in a deeply religious household on a farm in the American South. He had graduated from Bob Jones College in Tennessee and Wheaton College in Illinois – both Christian fundamentalist schools – and had a B.A. in anthropology.

We talked long and earnestly about my decision. Both of us sensed that, for all our avowed intentions to maintain our friendship, our feet were now set on divergent paths.

Later that summer, just before I enrolled at Princeton, we met again in New York City. On this occasion we spent the better part of two days closeted in a room in the Taft Hotel. All our differences came to a head in a discussion which, better than anything I know, explains Billy Graham and his phenomenal success as an evangelist.

In the course of our conversation I said, "But, Billy, it's simply not possible any longer to believe, for instance, the biblical account of creation. The world wasn't created over a period of days a few thousand years ago; it has evolved over millions of years. It's not a matter of speculation; it's demonstrable fact."

"I don't accept that," Billy said. "And there are reputable scholars who don't."

"Who are these scholars?" I said. "Men in conservative Christian colleges."

"Most of them, yes," he said. "But that's not the point. I believe the Genesis account of creation because it's in the Bible. I've discovered something in my ministry: when I take the Bible literally, when I proclaim it as the Word of God, my preaching has power. When I stand on the platform and say, 'God says,' or 'the Bible says,' the Holy Spirit uses me. There are results. Wiser men than you and I have been arguing questions like this for centuries. I don't have the time or the intellect to examine all sides of each theological dispute, so I've decided, once and for all, to stop questioning and accept the Bible as God's Word."

"But, Billy," I protested, "you can't do that. You don't dare stop thinking about the most important question in life. Do it and you begin to die. It's intellectual suicide."

"I don't know about anybody else," he said, "but I've decided that that's the path for me."

We talked about my going to Princeton and I pressed him to go with me. "Bill," I said, "face it. We've been successful in large part because of our abilities on the platform. Part of that stems from our energy, our convictions, our youth. But we won't always be young. We need to grow, to develop some intellectual sinew. Come with me to Princeton."

"I can't go to a university here in the States," he said. "I'm president of a Bible college, for goodness' sake!" He was – Northwestern Bible College, a fundamentalist school in Minneapolis.

"Resign," I said. "That's not what you're best fitted for; you're an evangelist. Come with me to Princeton."

There was an extended silence. Then, suddenly, he got up and came toward me. "Chuck," he said, "I can't go to a college here in the States. But I can and will do this: if we can get accepted by a university outside the country, maybe in England – Oxford, for instance – I'll go with you."

He stood in front of me, his hand outstretched. I know Billy well enough to know that, had I taken his hand, he would have kept his word. But I couldn't do it. I had resigned my church. I had been accepted at Princeton. The fall term was only weeks away. It was too late.

NOT MANY MONTHS later, Billy travelled to Los Angeles to begin the campaign that would catapult him overnight to international prominence. I have sometimes wondered what would have happened had I taken his hand that day. I am certain of this: he would not be the Billy Graham he has become, and the history of mass-evangelism would be quite different.

As was inevitable, Billy and I drifted apart. We often talked on the telephone and got together on occasion but, with the years, the occasions became fewer. One afternoon in the early 1970s he telephoned to say that he was in Toronto and suggested that he have dinner at my home. He wanted to meet my wife and children and to spend a long evening talking.

The evening ended earlier than planned; we simply ran out of subjects of mutual interest. As I drove him to his hotel in downtown Toronto, the conversation became desultory. On the drive home I felt a profound sense of sorrow. Marshall Frady in his book, *Billy Graham*, quotes Billy as saying to him:

> "I love Chuck to this very day. He's one of the few men I have ever loved in my life. He and I had been so close. But then, all of a sudden, our paths were parting. He began to be a little cool to me then. I think . . ." He pauses and then offers with a faint little smile, "I think that Chuck felt sorry for me."

It will sound unforgivably condescending, but I do. He has given up the life of unrestricted thought. I occasionally watch Billy in his televised campaigns. Forty years after our working together he is saying the same things, using the same phrases, following the same pattern. When he gives the invitation to come forward, the sequence, even the words, are the same. I turn off the set and am sometimes overtaken by sadness.

I think Billy is what he has to be. I disagree with him at almost every point in his views on God and Christianity and think that much of what he says in the pulpit is puerile, archaic nonsense. But there is no feigning in Billy Graham: he believes what he believes with an invincible innocence. He is the only mass-evangelist I would trust.

And I miss him.

AS MY FINAL YEAR at Princeton drew to a close, both the Presbyterian Church U.S.A. and the National Council of Christian Churches in the U.S.A. approached me. Princeton – as I had been warned – hadn't granted me a degree on my completion of the required courses, but the Philadelphia Presbytery moved to waive the academic qualification rule and ordain me. Shortly thereafter, Lafayette College (after representations were made by President Mackay) conferred on me an honorary Doctor of Divinity degree, "in recognition of his unique contribution to a balanced, intellectually sound and theologically based evangelism."

The approach by the National Council of Churches surprised and pleased me. The NCC represents most of the major American denominations: the Methodists, Presbyterians, Lutherans, and many others. Their offer was that I conduct, under their auspices, what they preferred to call preaching missions. I accepted, specifying three conditions: that there be no interference in what I would say, that three months of the year be spent preaching in my native Canada, and that the remuneration for me and my wife, combined, be $150 per week. Any surplus would be divided fifty-fifty between the local community and the National Council of Churches.

I had insisted that we receive a salary. Customarily, the evangelist is given all the money collected on the closing night of a campaign after an appeal has been made on his behalf. The "love offering" had long been something of a scandal.

The announcement of my appointment made news. *Time* magazine carried a feature story in the religion section and used the opportunity to shaft Billy. He had just completed a campaign in Atlanta, Georgia, and *Time* ran a picture of him with a mail-sack bulging with the "love offering" presented to him on the closing night. Billy, to his credit, immediately put himself on a salary.

I take some pride in the fact that I conducted the first integrated public meeting south of the Mason-Dixon line. The year was 1953 and the city was Richmond, Virginia. I was formally invited to conduct a city-wide campaign. I accepted, stipulating that the meetings would have to be unsegregated. The committee replied that this was not possible; there was a by-law prohibiting it. I wrote that, under the circumstances, I would have to withdraw my acceptance. Shortly thereafter I received a letter stating that, after pressure had been brought to bear by the Ministerial Association, the city council had granted permission.

I MOVED ACROSS THE United States and Canada for the next few years, conducting fifteen-day – three successive Sundays – preaching missions in the larger cities. In each city, records were set for attendance. But I was facing problems with my health. I was thirty-five and thought myself to be in perfect physical condition, but I had begun to suffer frequent pains in the chest. Oddly, the pain never troubled me while preaching, but mornings I would often find myself short of breath with a tightness in my chest and a numbness radiating to my forearms and fingers. During a campaign in Cincinnati, I went to see a doctor. He found no evidence of a problem with my heart.

But the symptoms didn't go away. Indeed, they seemed to be exacerbated by the difficulties I was having with my faith. The old doubts were resurfacing. I would cover them over with prayer and activity but soon there would be a wisp of smoke and a flicker of flame and then a firestorm of doubt. I would banish them only to have them return.

Part of the problem was that there was no one to talk to. How does a man who, each night, tells ten to twenty thousand people how to find faith confess that he is struggling with his own?

IRONICALLY, AT THE very moment I was trying to shore up my faith, there was a flurry of interest in me and my campaigns in the national media. We were cutting a new trail through the tangled underbrush of mass-evangelism and it was being noted in magazine articles and major newspaper features: among them *Time* and *Newsweek*, the *Chicago Sunday Tribune*, *Maclean's* magazine in Canada, the *Globe and Mail Magazine*, and a dozen other journals carried feature stories. The NBC television network asked me to do a series of four half-hour programs emanating from Chicago. *American Magazine* carried a major feature beginning:

> I have just seen the man who's giving religion a brand new look; a young Canadian by the name of Charles Templeton. Passing up the old hellfire-and-damnation oratorical fireworks, he uses instead an attractive, persuasive approach that presents religion as a commodity as necessary to life as salt, and in the doing, has set a new standard for mass evangelism.

Dispensing with such props as the "sawdust trail," the "Mourner's Bench" and other tricks from the old-fashioned evangelist's repertoire, he is winning converts at an average of 150 a night and – what is something new in modern evangelism – they stay converted. At a recent two-week campaign in Evansville, Indiana, for example, a count showed that Templeton had drawn a total attendance of 91,000 out of a population of 128,000. A survey six months later showed that church attendance was 17 percent higher than it had been before he came . . .

Six months later I was in Harrisburg, the capital of Pennsylvania, for what would be the most successful meeting we had yet seen. The days were filled with excitement but my nights were bedevilled by fear, by sudden sweats, and by a pounding of my heart that sometimes shook the bed. Mornings I endured the now familiar pains in my chest and arms. In desperation I sought out the man reputed to be the best coronary specialist in the state. I expected to hear the counsel I'd been given before: "Ease up. Take a vacation." Instead, he said, "There is nothing wrong with your heart. Nothing. The pains you get – let me put it in layman's language – originate in your head. There is something in your life that is troubling you. Some conflict. Whatever it is, deal with it. Otherwise, you will continue to feel your symptoms and will likely begin to see others."

After the closing service – described in the *Harrisburg Journal* as "the greatest crowd ever to gather in the history of Harrisburg" – I told my wife, during the drive back to New York City where we lived, "I'm going to leave the ministry."

But I temporized. The Presbyterian Church U.S.A. had been pressing me to take over its Department of Evangelism, not so much to preach as to lead the denomination toward a program of responsible evangelism. I had rejected their overtures, but now I accepted and, as Director of Evangelism, took over a suite of offices and a staff at Presbyterian headquarters on Fifth Avenue in New York City.

Over the next three years, I trained ministers and laymen, lectured in theological seminaries, wrote two books, and hosted a weekly television show, "Look Up and Live," on the CBS network. I continued occasionally to preach but only on Sundays as a guest, most frequently at Fifth Avenue Presbyterian Church.

And I struggled with my faith.

IT IS AN ANNUAL custom at Yale University to bring in a prominent preacher for a week of religious services. The guest speaks each weekday morning in the chapel and makes himself available through the day for interviews with students. In the spring of 1956 I was invited. Each morning, I donned a black gown and my Doctor of Divinity hood and, from the ornate stone pulpit, preached to the students. They filled the pews, sat on the floor, and spilled through the doors into the hallways.

The committee of students assigned to help me, members of the Student Christian Movement, came to me late in the week in high excitement. The outstanding man in the senior class had asked for an appointment. He was a member of a wealthy family, an honours student in political science, captain of the Yale debating team, and, from his sophomore year, quarterback of the football team.

We met in the office assigned to me during my stay. He began our discussion by saying, "Before we start, may we establish some ground rules? Otherwise, we may go around in circles."

I agreed, and he continued, "Then let me suggest that, if at any time you say something I disagree with, I be permitted to interrupt. Otherwise, if you then go on to build an argument on that position, it makes it difficult later on to take issue. A lot of time is wasted and a lot of confusion arises."

"I entirely agree," I said. "So long as the rule works both ways."

We talked for a full hour, each trying to score debating points. He was a resourceful debater but it was not difficult to counter his arguments. Theology was my discipline and I'd heard most of the points he raised dozens of times.

At the appointed time he rose to leave. "I want to thank you," he said. "You make a hell of a good case. I won't say you've convinced me, but what you said makes sense. I promise you I'll give it serious thought."

After he left, my first reaction was one of elation – I'd beaten the captain of the Yale debating team. I'd made my points with a sure-footedness acquired in dozens of such confrontations, not least in debates with myself. They were reasonable, intellectually acceptable arguments, but arguments that no longer convinced me.

The elation was replaced by self-reproach. The student was searching for direction in his life and it was possible that I had influenced him in a life-altering decision. What right did I have to meddle thus in his life? Indeed, what right did I have to stand before a student body or an assemblage of thousands and, using all the persuasive skills I had acquired with the years, seek to win them to something I was no longer sure of myself?

It was a reprehensible thing to do and that day I decided to stop.

Some six weeks later I resigned my post with the Presbyterian Church and submitted my resignation to the New York Presbytery. The Presbytery was charitable. They urged me to reconsider and moved not to accept my resignation for one year. To intensify the dilemma, representatives from the Fifth Avenue Presbyterian Church approached me about becoming their senior minister. The weekly television show I was doing on the CBS network was renewed and I was asked to continue as host. Having made the decision to go, I was being tempted to stay.

I had no idea what I would do. I owned no assets but my car and some $600 in savings. I was cutting myself off from the many friends I had made during my years in the ministry. I was abandoning people who looked to me for guidance, including thirty-six men and women who were in seminary or the ministry or on the mission field because of my influence. I felt like a betrayer.

But there was no real choice. I could stay in the ministry and live a lie or I could make the break. My wife and I packed our few possessions in a rented trailer and started on the road back to Toronto where, nineteen years earlier, I had begun.

The God Myth

Is There a God?

I am a former Christian minister who is now an agnostic – not an atheist, not a theist, not a sceptic, and certainly not indifferent. And because the precise meaning of these terms is frequently confused, let me clarify the distinctions between them.

The theist asserts that there is one God, that he is the creator and ruler of the universe, and that he can be encountered by faith. The Christian theist believes that God reveals himself to the individual through the study of his Word and the individual's acceptance of Jesus Christ as Saviour and Lord.

The atheist asserts that God does not exist, a conclusion as logically untenable as the contention that he does. One cannot prove that there *is* a God any more than one can prove that there *is not*, neither proposition being subject to proof. Both the theist and the atheist arrive at their antithetical conclusions not by a process of logic but by an act of faith.

The atheist insists that his conclusions are rational and have been arrived at after an examination of the available evidence. But such an assertion is unsupportable and presumptuous. Our world, our universe, and we ourselves comprise – to appropriate Winston Churchill's phrase in another context – "a riddle wrapped in a mystery inside an enigma" – and to assert unequivocally that we and the cosmos are the result of blind chance requires as great a leap of faith as that taken by the theist. Moreover, by insisting that there is no God, the atheist assumes the impossible task of proving a negative.

Atheism is essentially reactionary. It is a response to those who assert that there *is* a God. It may legitimately be argued that the universe is impersonal, indifferent, and without apparent purpose, but to insist that this is so is not to demonstrate it. It amounts to an abandonment of the inquiry.

HOW DOES THE AGNOSTIC differ from both the theist and atheist?

To begin, let it be clear that agnosticism is not a halfway house between theism and atheism. The agnostic does not say, as is commonly believed, "I do not know whether or not there is a God." He says, "I *cannot* know. There may have been a First Cause to which one might apply the name God, there may even be a Supreme Being from which all existence proceeds, but on the basis of the available evidence the question is beyond resolution."

Is this quibbling? Hardly. If the existence of God is not demonstrable except by faith, and if there is no hard evidence that the universe was created by a First Cause, then agnosticism is the only rational position.

The agnostic asserts that, rather than the Word of God, the Holy Bible is only one of many holy books in which various peoples at various times in human history have set down their beliefs about the source of being and the meaning and purpose of life.

The agnostic asserts further that the Old Testament is simply the compilation of various attempts by a Middle Eastern Semitic people (the Jews) to preserve in written form their beliefs about the nature of their God, his creation of the world, and his dealings with his "Chosen People."

He asserts that the New Testament is essentially the collected record of the conclusions of a number of Palestinian Jews concerning Jesus of Nazareth, including their belief that he was the Son of God, the Second Person of the Holy Trinity.

He asserts that a combination of historic circumstances has made Christianity the dominant religion of the Western world but that it is not unique, there being a host of other religions and a variety of other deities worshipped or revered by millions of men and women in various parts of the world.

As to whether or not there is a God, one may not simply beg the question by saying, "I *cannot* know." This is an intellectual cop-out, a failure to attempt within the limits of one's ability to seek an answer to what is surely the ultimate question. One may not legitimately say, "I *cannot* know," unless one has *sought* to know.

ONE OF THE FIRST THINGS learned by anyone who seeks an answer to the riddle of the universe is that, while chance may play a part, our lives, our world, and the universe are not governed by chance. They do appear, however, to be governed by what may best be described as laws – physical, moral, and spiritual laws.

Certainly this is true of the physical world. Gravity may be defined as the mutual attraction between all matter, but it is so much more than this. The law of gravity makes mobility possible. Obey the law of gravity and you are free, in normal circumstances, to move about as you will. But disobedience of the law of gravity is not an option – you *must* obey it or suffer the consequences.

The bones and musculature of humankind have evolved as they have in obedience to the law of gravity, the end result being the ability to stand upright, to walk, to run, even to fly. Across many millennia our forebears learned how to adapt to the law and use it for their benefit. *Homo erectus* learned to stand and walk upright because he discovered that by doing so he was able to see farther – the better to discern prey or an enemy. Centuries later the Wright brothers learned to break the bonds of earth in their flying machine not by disregarding the law of gravity but by using it.

But in addition to the physical laws there are laws that apply even to our thoughts. Your brain, for example: you must use it or lose it – it's the law. Your muscles: exercise them or they will atrophy – it's the law. The operation of these universal laws can be observed even in such intangible matters as human relationships: love and you will be loved; hate and you will be hated. And they function at every level: overeat and you will put on weight; starve and you will wither and die. It's the law. You smile a smile out of a baby. Pat a dog and it will wag its tail, kick it and it will bite you. It's the law.

We learn the laws of life by living. They are built into the universe.

They are built into us. Observe them and you will benefit from them. Break them and you break yourself on them.

The laws of life that affect our daily lives are not revealed truths communicated by a deity on a smoking mountain or delivered through some special compact into the hands of priests or rabbis or members of the clergy; they lie at the heart of life. The philosopher discovers them in his pondering and passes them on. The scientist tracks them down in his laboratory and passes them on. The novelist observes them in his scrutiny of human behaviour and passes them on. The poet intuits them in his meditation and passes them on. There is no need to petition the gods, to erect costly temples, to follow elaborate forms of worship, or to sanctify ordinary men on the presumption that by virtue of their vocation they have special access to the truth. The laws of life are intrinsic in everything that exists and are available to anyone.

The Christian church speaks about "revealed truth," but the only revealed truth is that which breaks upon the mind as the result of cognition. Learning – coming to awareness, arriving at conclusions, synthesizing them – proceeds from feeding information to the brain.

The philosophers, the scientists, the artists, and the seers are the real revealers of truth. The philosopher arrives at his insights by observing life and synthesizing information, the scientist by examining data, the artist by capturing visible, audible, or tactile beauty and communicating it through sculpture or painting or writing or music. The seer contemplates the essence of reality and in so doing catches a glimpse of life's meaning and the human potential.

It is through this awareness of ourselves and others that we discover ways to live abundantly, to understand and co-operate with others, even to love one another.

I do not denigrate holy books such as the Bible, the Torah, or the Koran, or the men who wrote them. They contain gems of early wisdom, profound insights, but they should be recognized for what they are – not the revealed word of a deity but the conclusions and insights of men and women who, across the centuries, have sought to understand and explain the mysteries of existence.

Some of these insights are timeless, but in early history most were uninformed and primitive. Our early forebears sought within the limits of their experience to interpret life's imponderables, usually attributing the inexplicable to the intervention of one or more of their gods, demi-deities, and evil spirits who, they believed, controlled not only the physical world but life and destiny. Even today – for all that they know better – insurance companies still attribute natural catastrophes, aberrations in the weather, accidents or events beyond human control, to "acts of God."

But surely, as we approach the twenty-first century it is time to have done with primitive speculation and superstition and look at life in rational terms. We are in large measure the masters of our fate – subject, of course, to our genetic inheritance, mental illness, accident or disease – and we are all equipped to ponder the eternal questions, explore the unknown, and examine the *mysterium tremendum* secure in the knowledge that in doing so we are not going counter to "the will of God" and will not bring on ourselves the vengeful wrath of some punctilious deity because we rejected or failed to observe some arcane prohibition.

An Abundance of Gods

Contemplate the Christian idea that there is one God. Then consider for a moment how many gods there are and have been through the ages; their number is in the thousands. Some have disappeared as civilization and the larger world religions have made inroads, but across the centuries gods have been as numerous and their places of origin as various as the imagination of their creators.

Every nation or tribe or people in history has worshipped a god or gods of some kind. Many of these gods are unique, some are part of a pantheon. Some have human form, some animal. Some have a number of arms. Some have more than one head. Some have wings. Some are local and limited in their ability; others – including the Hebrew/ Christian God – are omnipotent, omniscient, and ubiquitous. Some of the gods are depicted as naked. Others are elaborately adorned, with robes, necklaces and bracelets of precious stones, even with entwined snakes. Some *are* snakes. Some are armed: with sword and shield, buckler, dagger, or club.

Some live in the heavens, others in the sea or the forest. Some breathe fire. One holds lightning bolts in his mouth.

Some are male, some female, some neither, some both. Some are the spirits of dead ancestors. Some transform themselves at will into men, women, swans, bulls, doves. Some communicate through thunder and lightning, tempest and storm, through inscribed tablets of stone, through hurricane and earthquake, by pillars of fire and cloud.

Most of the gods are intensely parochial: they hate every people but their own. They are jealous, vengeful, given to punishing the wicked – especially, the disobedient – even to the third and fourth generation.

Most are utter egotists and insist on frequent praise and flattery. They are jealous of rival gods and often curse those who worship them. Some require the presentation of gifts, sometimes demanding the sacrifice of an animal, an enemy, a child, or a virgin. Their perfume is the smoke from sacrificial altars and the scent of blood, especially the blood of those who worship other gods.

Some are distant and remain aloof; others make love to humans. Some have children by them.

Most of the gods require unquestioning obedience. They are pleased when men confess their failures, especially when, while doing so, they prostrate themselves, put their foreheads in the dust of the ground, cover themselves with ashes, berate and demean themselves.

Most appoint representatives, commonly called priests and almost always men. These exclusive representatives usually organize themselves into a hierarchy. Their duty, they insist, is to see that ordinary men and women obey every jot and tittle of the demands made on them by the deity and communicated through them. These priests usually require – in the deity's name – abject and unquestioning obedience and, by way of offerings, the best of whatever is available, whether it be food, wine, currency, precious metals, exotic stones, or elaborate edifices.

Is it credible that, had you been born in Asia or Afghanistan or the Antipodes or Amazonia or elsewhere, you would believe what you do today?

We worship the gods of our predecessors.

The Various Religions

Christianity is based on the premise that the Bible is the Word of God, that the Creator of the universe has revealed his purpose and his will through his "Chosen People," the Jews and, fully, through the life and teaching of Jesus of Nazareth, "his only begotten son."

The Old Testament is taken to be the record of God's creation of the universe and his dealings with his Chosen People, Israel. The New Testament is the story of the incarnation of God in Jesus of Nazareth, of Jesus' teachings, his life and death and the beginnings of the Christian church.

Living in the West, where the dominant religions are Christianity and Judaism, we tend to forget that, over the centuries, there have been hundreds of religions and thousands of gods, gods as varied as the people who gave them birth and, inevitably, reflecting their culture.

The religions of some of the peoples on Planet Earth are complex and profound, others are relatively simple, others are primitive. Some worship no god. The Australian aboriginal, for example, practises magic and fetishism but does not consider the powers involved to be supernatural. Many peoples see their gods at work in such events as the fall of a tree that kills a man or in a flood or famine. They do not always personalize such forces but may seek to counter them through activities such as ritual dances, the mutilation of their bodies, or various sacred rites.

Emerging modern man began to make distinctions between natural and supernatural forces. This led to acts of propitiation and, inevitably, to self-appointed experts and arbiters: medicine-men or priests who claimed to have the ability to influence the gods, control nature's aberrations, and drive off false gods, demons, and evil spirits.

In parts of the world, some deities and nature gods are identified with natural phenomena. Examples: the Egyptian sun god, Ra; the Babylonian goddess of fertility, Ishtar; the Greek sea god, Poseidon; and the Hindu goddess of destruction and death, Kali.

Other faiths adopt such concepts as the dualism of the Zoroastrians, in which there are equally powerful deities of good and evil; the polytheism of the Hindus and Greeks, in which there are many gods; the pantheism of the Manichaeans, in which God is identified with the universe and the universe with God.

Some faiths are categorized as "revealed" religions: Judaism, for example, in which Yahweh reveals the Ten Commandments; Christianity, in which Jesus reveals the will of the Father; and Islam, in which the angel Gabriel reveals the will of God to Muhammad.

Some religions are the result of human inquiry and the development of what have been described as "philosophies of eternity." Among these are Buddhism, Brahmanism, Taoism, and other Asian metaphysical belief systems. The Buddha and Muhammad, it should be noted, are not deities but enlightened leaders.

The deity we are discussing in these pages is the God of the Jews, called, severally, Jehovah, Elohim, Yahweh, and, among Christians, God the Father, Jesus Christ, the Son, and the Holy Ghost.

IT IS IMPERATIVE TO keep in mind that the universe as we understand it and the universe that Jews and early Christians conceived of are utterly dissimilar. When, in the book of Genesis, God creates the heavens and the earth, the authors envision the universe as a three-tiered entity entirely under the authority and personal control of God the Father. These are:

- Heaven: the abode of Yahweh and his angels and near enough to be reached by erecting a tower, as was done in Babel.

- Earth, the middle realm: God the Father's creation over a period of six days; the dwelling place of humankind and the various creatures God created.
- Sheol, Hell, the nether world, the grave.

The earth was assumed by Jews and early Christians to be flat, overarched by the dome of Heaven and, with Heaven, comprising the universe. The sun, moon, and stars were mere lights in the vault that separated Heaven from the earth and contained the water that fell from time to time as rain or hail or snow. The Israelites believed that they alone were God's Chosen People. Chosen or not, the common people did not themselves have direct access to God. He could be approached only by their leaders or by a special group, priests, who acted as interpreters of the Law and as mediators between God and men.

There were numerous other gods at the time, many more than there were tribes. Most of these gods were jealous of one another, warred with one another, manifested human characteristics, and occasionally assumed human or animal form. They talked to men, argued with them on occasion, and were sometimes subject to persuasion. The God of the Hebrews, Yahweh, was a typical tribal god. He was mercurial in temperament, given to rages, punctilious about the various prescribed ceremonies, and meticulous to the point of fussiness about such minutiae as the fringes on priestly garments, the techniques for slaughtering and preparing blood sacrifices, and on and interminably on. Yahweh approved slavery and polygamy. To achieve his objectives for his Chosen People, he could – and often did – order the killing of every inhabitant in an alien city, men, women, children, even animals. In the Genesis story of the Great Flood, he drowned the entire population of the world except for one family. And he frequently subjected the world to earthquakes, volcanos, hurricanes, droughts, plagues, and diseases, using these from time to time to punish disobedience.

IN THE WESTERN WORLD, most of the millions of men and women who call themselves Christians take it for granted that there is a God in Heaven and that Jesus, "the Father's only begotten son," came to earth to reveal the Father's will and die for their sins. They believe further that theirs is the only true faith and that their God cares for them through each day and will receive them into Heaven when they die.

The great majority of men and women in the world do not believe this. Their heritage being different, they have a different world-view, different ideas about God, different legends about how the universe and the world came into being, different concepts about the meaning and purpose of life, and different beliefs about what happens when they die.

Not surprisingly, they believe that Christians are infidels and that the claims made by the Christian church are an affront to their god.

CHRISTIANS ARE A SMALL minority in the world. Approximately four of every five people on the face of the earth believe in gods other than the Christian God. The more than five billion people who live on earth revere or worship more than three hundred gods. If one includes the animist or tribal religions, that number rises to more than three thousand.

Are we to believe that only Christians are right?

Christians need to remember that their beliefs came to them from the Jews. They inherited their concept of God from Israel and expanded it to include the worship of Jesus of Nazareth as God, a practice most Jews regard as blasphemy.

In New Testament times the Jews were a relatively small group of Semitic people living mostly in a forbidding land at the eastern end of the Mediterranean. It was their belief that their god was the only true god and that the gods worshipped by their neighbours were all false. Christians, having superimposed on Judaism the Christian faith, have the temerity to insist that there is only one God – theirs – and that the gods of every other people on earth are spurious! The apostle Paul stated it bluntly in a letter he wrote to the Christian community at Ephesus: "There is no other name under heaven, given among men, by which you may be saved; for there is salvation in no other."

Such insufferable presumption! And consider the implications:

Paul is asserting that anyone in the world who does not worship his God is damned forever! But let common sense rule for a moment: is it reasonable to believe that if the Creator of all the earth and the Father of all mankind wanted to reveal himself and his will to the men and women of the world he would do so only to a tiny group of Mediterranean people, leaving the remainder of the world in ignorance?

But many Christians *do* believe and teach this. They believe that, apart from their God, all men and women live in pagan darkness. Indeed, it is this conviction that provides the motivation for Christians in their efforts to get the gospel message out. Even more incredibly, Christians believe that the failure to accept Jesus Christ as Saviour and Lord is to be consigned at death to an endless hell.

The implication of this belief is clear: it is that the vast majority of the men, women, and children who have lived on earth are in Hell suffering endless torment and will remain in this condition forever.

To believe this is to make the Christian God a monster beyond imagining. Any intelligent human being will recognize that the concept is incredible. Yet it is the clear teaching of the New Testament.

The Bible versus the Facts

We should approach the teaching of the Bible as we would any other data – with objectivity. Inasmuch as our unique human heritage includes the ability to reason, we should bring this ability to such questions as may arise in an examination of our religious beliefs. And we should arrive at whatever conclusions we reach on the grounds of the information available, rejecting both the scornful dismissal of the atheist and the willingness of the fundamentalist to believe anything.

At this point in history, this much is clear: it is no longer possible to have confidence in what the Christian church has to say about the origin and meaning of life – not least because there *is* no such thing as "The Church." There are, in fact, hundreds of churches, denominations, sects, communions, brotherhoods, companies of believers, and what have you, each disagreeing with the others on various points of doctrine, forms of worship, biblical interpretation, rituals, sacraments, and prohibitions.

We were told by our parents or preachers or Sunday-school teachers that God created the world in six days and rested on the seventh. And, indeed, that is what the Genesis account says. But every physicist in the world will tell you that such a view is nonsense; that it took billions of years for the universe, our galaxy, our solar system, and our world to evolve to its present and, it should be added, transitory form.

Whom should you believe, the theologians or the physicists?

29

We are told in the Bible that a few thousand years ago God created the first man and the first woman and placed them in a garden called Eden, and that every human being in history has descended from that first couple. But every anthropologist in the world will tell you that this is nonsense. Fossil remains indicate incontrovertibly that our earliest ancestors did not suddenly appear fully formed, but were anthropoid creatures who lived on the earth millions of years ago.

Whom should you believe on the question, the theologians or the anthropologists?

We are told by the Christian church that the Creator drove an accursed Adam and Eve out of an accursed Eden into an accursed world because they disobeyed one of his commandments, and that as a consequence all their descendants through all time were "born in sin and conceived in iniquity," and that this is the reason for all the crime, poverty, suffering, and general wickedness in the world. But every geneticist in the world will tell you that this is nonsense.

Whom should you believe on the question, the theologians or the geneticists?

One cannot help but wonder why, when Plan One went awry, God didn't learn from experience – as humans do – and have another go at creating the world, compensating for the blunders he made the first time. Surely this would have been better than throwing up his hands and cursing everybody and everything everywhere forever!

We have been told that, a few generations after Eden, God got angry when each new generation disobeyed his edicts, so he sent a devastating flood that covered the earth to the tops of the highest mountains and drowned every living creature with the exception of one family and pairs of each animal species. But every geologist in the world will tell you that there is no evidence whatsoever of a worldwide flood of such magnitude.

Whom should you believe on the subject, the theologians or the geologists?

We are told that, approximately two thousand years ago, a young unmarried woman, living in a small town in the Middle East, was made pregnant by God himself and that her child was, in fact, Almighty God, the Second Person of the Holy Trinity; that he travelled ancient Palestine as an itinerant preacher, performing numerous miracles and even raising the dead. We are told that he was arrested by the Roman government and executed by crucifixion and has not been seen since. The Christian church insists that he rose from the grave and ascended into Heaven.

Whom should you believe, the Christian church or your own common sense?

Racial Prejudice in the Bible

*I*n Sunday school when I was a child our teacher opened her Bible and read a verse from the New Testament, John 3:16. "This," she said, "is the best-known and best-loved verse in the Bible. It has been called the Gospel in a Nutshell":

> For God so loved the world that he gave his only begotten Son, that whosoever believeth in him should not perish but have everlasting life.

It did not occur to me until years later that, perhaps better than any other verse in the Bible, John 3:16 makes it clear that the Christian God is *not* the God of all the world.

If God's love encompasses the whole world and if everyone who does not believe in him will perish, then surely this question needs to be asked: When, after two thousand years, does God's plan kick in for the billion people he "so loves" in China? Or for the 840 million in India? Or the millions in Japan, Afghanistan, Siberia, Egypt, Burma . . . and on and on?

Why would a God who "so loved the world" reveal his message only to a tiny minority of the people on earth, leaving the majority in ignorance? Is it possible to believe that the Father of all Mankind would select as his Chosen People a small Middle Eastern nation, Israel, reveal his will exclusively to them, fight alongside them in their battles to survive, and only after their failure to reach out to any other group, update his plan for the world's salvation by sending his "only begotten son," not to the world but, once again, exclusively to Israel?

One should recognize the evident fact that Yahweh in the Old Testament and Jesus of Nazareth in the New were not concerned about the world as a whole. Throughout Israel's history Yahweh showed no interest in any people but his Chosen People, the Jews. Indeed, his only contact with the other Middle Eastern nations of that time was actively to help the Israelites conquer them in war.

It is difficult for Christians to acknowledge this, but it is the clear message of the scriptures: Yahweh was not the God of all mankind, he was a parochial deity and racially prejudiced. He was the God of Israel and the enemy of anyone and everyone who stood in their way. And the same was true of Jesus. Jesus directed his message not to the whole world but exclusively to the Jews. Having chosen his twelve apostles (all Jews) and having given them what has been called the "Great Commission," he added these specific instructions:

> Go nowhere among the Gentiles and enter no town of the Samaritans; but go rather to the lost sheep of the House of Israel and preach as you go, saying: 'The Kingdom of Heaven is at hand.'

And his actions matched his words. When Jesus was preaching in the district of Tyre and Sidon:

> And behold, a Canaanite woman from the region came out and cried, "Have mercy on me, Lord, Son of David; my daughter is tormented by a demon." But he did not answer her a word. And his disciples came and urged him, saying, "Send her away, for she keeps shouting after us." He answered. "I was sent only to the lost sheep of the house of Israel." But she came and knelt before him, saying, "Lord, help me." He answered, "It is not fair to take the children's food and throw it to the dogs." She said, "Yes, Lord, yet even the dogs eat the crumbs that fall from

their masters' table." Then Jesus answered her, "Woman, great
is your faith! Let it be done for you as you wish." And her
daughter was healed instantly.

It is a profoundly troubling passage. If Yahweh is, in Job's phrase,
"the breath of *all* mankind," and if he "so loved the world," why did
he evidence such bias – sending his message of life to Israel only and
then, through Jesus of Nazareth, almost exclusively to Jewish
Christians? Indeed, he seems to have been completely indifferent to
the needs of the majority of the people on earth.

It is clear: Jesus' mission was to the Jews and, with only rare
exceptions (the much-married Samaritan woman at the well in Sychar
and a Roman centurion who sought him out on behalf of his sick
servant), he made no effort to reach non-Jews. After his death, his disciples did broaden their mission to include those they described as
"the uncircumcised." And this exclusivist attitude has not changed
with the years. Contemporary Jews will accept Christians only if they
are converted to Judaism and Christians will accept Jews only if
they convert.

The God of the
Old Testament

The Creation

"*I*n the beginning God created the heavens and the earth . . ."
These are perhaps the most familiar words in the history of
Western civilization. They form the opening sentence in the Jewish
Torah and the Christian Bible and are fundamental to both traditional
Jewish and Christian beliefs.

In Genesis, the first book of the Bible, in a dramatic series of events
spanning six days, God is represented as creating the heavens, the
earth, animal and vegetable life, and, finally, the first man and
woman. Is there anyone in the Western world who has not from
childhood seen vividly in his or her imagination the dramatic
sequence of events described in the first two chapters of the Bible? The
naked and pristine first humans, the temptation by the serpent, the
eating of the fruit of the Tree of the Knowledge of Good and Evil,
God's curse and the expulsion from Paradise, the murder of Abel by
his brother Cain, the survival of Noah and his family during the Great
Flood, God's covenant with Abraham, the enslavement of the
Israelites in Egypt, God's call to Moses from the burning bush, the
Egyptian plagues, the slaughter of the Egyptian children in the dead
of night, the dramatic parting of the Red Sea and the destruction of
the Egyptian army, the wandering of the Israelites in the wilderness,
the handing down of the Ten Commandments in the smoke and thunder of Sinai, and, at long last, Israel's entry into the Promised Land.

They are enthralling tales and across the centuries they have made
an indelible impression on countless millions of men and women. But

are they history? Or are they no more than the traditions of a Middle
Eastern Semitic tribe and best categorized as folklore?

An unbiased reading of the biblical account will clearly show that,
while some of the events described in the early books of the Old
Testament may have been based on historic events, most are simply
embellished folk tales.

THE CREATION STORY IS an attempt by its authors to validate
Israel's view of itself as unique among humankind – God's Chosen
People. The astonishing part of the story is that, millennia later, millions of men and women, Jew and gentile alike, continue to accept the
biblical accounts of the Creation as fact even while acknowledging the
evidence of science that the universe had its beginnings billions of
years ago and that genus *Homo* has been around for at least 2.6 million years.

There are, of course, reasons why many cling to the biblical
account of the Creation and the Fall of Man: it has been from childhood the rock on which their concept of God, sin, redemption, and
life after death is based.

My purpose in these pages is not to denigrate Christian or Jewish
beliefs – they are part of the bedrock on which our society has been
built – but rather to make it clear that it is no longer possible for an
informed man or woman to believe that, for all its ancient wisdom,
its remarkable insights, and its occasional literary excellence, the
Bible is either a reliable account of our origins as human beings or, as
the Christian church insists, the infallible Word of God. The ancient
lore of the Old Testament and much of the teaching of Jesus of
Nazareth in the New may contribute to the fashioning of a useful philosophy of life, but they are anything but the definitive word on the
origin, the meaning, and the purpose of human existence.

LET US BEGIN THEN AT the beginning, with the Creation story
in the book of Genesis or, more accurately, with the Creation *stories*, for there are two, each differing from the other at almost every
point. So many and so fundamental are the intrinsic contradictions
that it is impossible to reconcile them. Even the deities involved are

different. In the first story God is, in the Hebrew, *Elohim*, in the second, *Yahweh*.

The first account is found in Genesis 1:1 through 2:3. The deity is Elohim. The earth is a void, a dark, fathomless sea. Elohim begins by separating the night from the day.

On Day Two he divides the waters in two with a vault above, calling the vault Heaven.

On Day Three he commands dry land to appear, calling the land Earth and the waters seas. He then creates vegetation: seed-bearing plants and fruit-bearing trees.

On Day Four he says, "Let there be lights in the vault of Heaven, a great light to govern the day [the sun] and a lesser light [the moon] to govern the night." And about time! There have already been three sunrises.

On Day Five he makes the seas teem with "sea serpents and every kind of fish" and turns the space between the earth and the vault of Heaven into a habitat "for every kind of winged creature."

Day Six – *The Big One!* Elohim has warmed up by creating the domestic animals, the birds, the wild beasts, and the reptiles. He now, it would seem, enlists some aid. The text reads: "And let *us* make man in *our* own image, after *our* likeness, and let them be dominant over every other living creature. [Italics mine]" And he does this, giving the man mastery over all other creatures and ordering him to mate and multiply.

"And Elohim saw everything that he had made, and behold it was very good."

This, according to the scriptures, is how the earth and life on earth began.

BUT HOLD ON A MOMENT! It isn't. Four verses into the second chapter of Genesis we come upon a second Creation story, a completely different story, even a different God! In version one he is Elohim. In version two he is Yahweh. And the second version differs from the first at every point. Rather than "a formless void, a dark fathomless sea," as in version one, the earth is described as a desert, barren of vegetation and without water, "for the Lord God had not caused it to rain on the earth, and there was not a man to till the ground. . . . And the Lord God formed man of the dust of the ground, and breathed into his nostrils the breath of life; and man became a living soul." There is no mention of a woman, an animal, a bird, a fish, or "a creeping thing."

Yahweh then plants a garden in Eden and fills it with every kind of tree. Among them – and here's the thorn on the rose! – the Tree of Life and the Tree of the Knowledge of Good and Evil. The man is placed in the garden, told to cultivate it and given a warning: "Of every tree in the garden thou mayest freely eat: but of the Tree of the Knowledge of Good and Evil thou shalt not eat of it: For on the day that thou eatest thereof thou shalt surely die."

At this point, belatedly realizing that "it is not good that the man should be alone," Yahweh says, "I will make him an helpmeet for him." Whereupon he does a very strange thing. The text says: "Out of the ground the Lord God formed every beast of the field and every fowl of the air and brought them unto Adam to see what he would call them."

It would seem, on the face of it, that Yahweh's intention was that one of the animals be the man's mate, for the story continues: "But for Adam there was not found an help meet for him." So, "the Lord God caused a deep sleep to fall upon Adam. And he took one of his ribs and closed up the flesh instead thereof; And the rib that the Lord God had taken from man, made he a woman and brought her unto the man."

Whereupon Adam said, "This is now bone of my bones and flesh of my flesh: she shall be called wo-*man* because she was taken out of man."

The story then concludes: "And the man and his wife were both naked and were not ashamed."

NOTE THE FUNDAMENTAL disparities in the two Creation stories:

- In the first story the God is *Elohim*. In the second he is *Yahweh*.
- In the first story the earth is described as covered with water, and it is not until the third day that Yahweh commands dry land to

appear. In the second story the earth is a barren desert, without any water "save for a mist that rose from the land."

- In the first story, Elohim divides the waters of the earth, sustains the upper waters with a vault and names the space above it, Heaven. In the second there is no such separation and no mention of a Heaven.
- In the first story, Elohim separates the light from the darkness, thus establishing the first day. Paradoxically, he doesn't create the sun or the moon until Day Four.
- In the first story, having created the birds, animals, and sea creatures, Elohim creates a man and a woman. In the second story Yahweh *begins* by creating a man, forming him from the dust of the ground. He then creates the Tree of Life and the Tree of the Knowledge of Good and Evil. It should be noted that although the fruit of the second tree is the cause of Adam's fall from grace it is not so much as mentioned by Elohim.
- In the second story, Yahweh, having decided to provide a helpmate for the man, proceeds to create, not a woman, but the animals. Then, when no helpmate suitable for man was found, Yahweh *fashioned*, rather than *created*, a woman, forming her from one of the man's ribs.
- The first story ends happily, with Elohim giving the man and the woman dominance over every living thing, and concludes with the words, "And God saw every thing that he had made, and behold it was very good."

Whereupon, he rested from his labours on the seventh day.

THEN, SUDDENLY, A monumental disaster! A talking snake, described as "more subtil than any beast of the field which the Lord God had made," comes to the woman and says, "Yea, hath God said, Ye shall not eat of every tree of the garden?"

And the woman said unto the serpent, "We may eat of the fruit of the trees of the garden: but of the fruit of the tree which is in the midst of the garden, God hath said, Ye shall not eat of it, neither shall ye touch it lest ye die." And the serpent said unto the woman, "Ye shall not surely die: for God doth know that in the day ye eat thereof, then your eyes shall be opened and ye shall be as gods, knowing good and evil."

And when the woman saw that the tree was good for food, and that it was pleasant to the eyes, and a tree to be desired to make one wise, she took of the fruit thereof, and did eat, and gave also her husband with her; and he did eat. And the eyes of them both were opened, and they knew that they were naked; and they sewed fig leaves together, and made themselves aprons.

And now the denouement. Later, they heard the voice of the Lord God walking in the garden in the cool of the day:

and Adam and his wife hid themselves from the presence of the Lord God amongst the trees of the garden. And the Lord God called unto Adam, and said unto him, "Where art thou?"

And he said, "I heard thy voice in the Garden, and I was afraid because I was naked; and I hid myself."

And he said, "Who told thee that thou wast naked? Hast thou eaten of the tree, whereof I commanded thee that thou shouldest not eat?"

And the man said, "The woman whom thou gavest to be with me, she gave me of the tree and I did eat."

And the Lord God said unto the woman, "What is this that thou hast done?" And the woman said, "The serpent beguiled me, and I did eat."

Whereupon Yahweh lays a curse on the serpent, the man, and the woman, fashions clothing for the man and woman from the skins of animals, and, lest they eat of the Tree of Life and live forever, banishes them from the garden, cursing the soil of all the earth and informing the man that he will subsist by the sweat of his brow until he returns to the dust from which he was formed.

He then posts cherubims at the east of the Garden of Eden and a flaming sword which turned every way to guard the way to the Tree of Life.

AS IS OBVIOUS, THE stories are fables, attempts to explain how the world and its various life forms came into being and why life is imperfect. But, juvenile and contradictory as these folk tales are, they have remained the grounds of Christian theology across the centuries. They purport to explain man's existence and his sinfulness, nature's variety and its jeopardies, and all suffering and death.

But surely no contemporary man or woman can continue to hold to a world view based on these ancient and primitive folk tales. They may have sufficed for a people living in a time when men and women knew nothing of the cosmos and little about the laws that govern it and needed for their peace of mind plausible explanations for the mysteries of life and death, nature's bounty and its frequent jeopardy, and the ten thousand imponderables that are a part of life.

But from our vantage point, we know that nature is not whimsical, that the laws that govern life are not capricious, that humankind did not emerge fully formed from the dust of the ground but has evolved over millions of years, that our world is not the centre of the universe, that the heavens are not shaped like an inverted bowl, that the cosmos is not random but orderly and apparently without limits, that sickness and death are not the punishment of a crotchety and sometimes cruel deity, and that the disposition to challenge accepted wisdom is not sinful but is the very ability that makes us unique among the creatures of earth.

Surely it is a negation of human experience and intellectual and scientific progress to cling to the archaic and untenable notion that the universe and our lives are the creation of and in the control of a primitive tribal deity, a male chauvinist much given to anger, intolerance, and fits of pique when crossed.

Moreover, if God is, as the Christian church teaches, omniscient, if he exists apart from time and knows the future, would he not know before he created the world that the experiment would end in disaster?

The question then becomes: if he knows the end from the beginning, why go through the exercise? If his goal was to create an intelligent species and set it down in a paradise, why would he load the dice against his new creatures by creating a wily talking snake, which was, the Genesis story says, "more subtil than any beast of the field which the Lord God had made"?

Unless the deity is Machiavellian or obtuse, none of this makes sense.

Equally incredible is the fact that, having created the man and the woman, God forbids them to eat from the Tree of the Knowledge of Good and Evil, being fully aware, as he presumably would be, that should they do so they would acquire the ability to distinguish between right and wrong and, in this respect, "be as the gods." How naive of the omniscient deity not to know that, given the opportunity, they would seize it. Surely the ability to discriminate between options is a desirable trait and one to be coveted?

If God is omniscient, would he not know that giving the man and the woman the ability to think but not to reason made them little different from the animals? So why trouble to create them? The assertion by the serpent that God wanted to withhold from Adam and Eve the power to reason because he knew that with it they would be like the gods suggests that the serpent already had the ability to reason. Quite clearly he knew the difference between right and wrong and was out to frustrate God's purposes.

Furthermore, if God has a need to be worshipped, and across the centuries he has insisted on it – on pain of eternal death! – he is not going to satisfy the need by creating a man and a woman incapable of choice. If they have no choice *but* to worship the Creator, what satisfaction could there be for God in that? Worship from a fawning automaton would not be worth having. For worship to have value it must proceed from a creature who has the ability to withhold it and then chooses to offer it. Without the ability to make rational choices a man is not a man, he is one of the lesser creatures – and God had already created enough of them.

And what is this consuming need the God of the Bible has to be worshipped, to be everlastingly praised and assured that he is the Great One, the most deserving of adoration and praise?

Today such a condition would be diagnosed as pathological.

SUPPOSE I WERE TO GO to my workshop and make a toy, so fashioning it that when a switch is thrown it will genuflect and say, "Oh mighty Creator, I worship and adore you. You are wise beyond all others and the embodiment of loving kindness. Praise be to your name." The toy continues to do this until, tiring of the adulation, I turn the switch off. Would an onlooker not wonder, "What overwhelming insecurity does this man have that he needs – indeed, takes great pains to get – such meaningless flattery?"

Yet, across the centuries, the God of the Bible has required – on pain of endless suffering and death – such fawning compliments. When he created the first man and woman he instructed them to be fruitful and multiply and replenish the earth, filling it with descendants whose primary duty would be to worship their Creator. He then went on to command these people to erect costly temples, establish elaborate rituals, slay and burn animals on altars, bring their possessions and put them in the hands of a group of lackeys known as priests, whose primary responsibility was to remind the people of the deity's demands and see to it that every jot and tittle of their worship is done in precisely the way the deity wants it done.

Or else!

Is it possible for any contemporary person to believe that God, being omniscient and knowing in advance that his Garden of Eden experiment would end in disaster, nevertheless went ahead with it? This is even more difficult to accept when one contemplates the chaotic result of it all: the cursing of the man, the woman, and every other creature, the banishing of his newly minted couple from Eden and the introduction on earth of a population predisposed to wickedness: men and women who, within a few generations, will have become so universally nasty and brutish that it will be necessary to send a flood to – in Yahweh's words – "wipe them off the face of the earth."

NOTE THAT, IN THE Genesis account, the Creator is utterly unlike the omniscient and loving God of Christian theology:

- He is inept: His master plan for an Edenic paradise goes awry from the beginning.
- He lacks foresight: His original intention was that Adam mate with one of the animals; the woman was an afterthought.
- He is unjust: He curses not only the man and woman but all their unborn descendants for what was inevitable given the nature he himself had created in them.
- He is vindictive: He tells the woman, "Because of what you have done, I will make child-bearing painful for you. And, to ensure your punishment, I will cause you to lust for your husband."
- He is gender-biased: He tells the woman that her role will be one of subservience to her husband. "He will lord it over you."
- He is not omniscient: Out for an evening stroll in the garden, he seems to have no idea where the first man and woman are hiding and has to ask where they are and what they have been up to.
- He is subject to fatigue: The Sabbath was instituted because, as the Genesis record specifies: "God rested on the seventh day after all the work he had been doing."

BEFORE CONCLUDING THIS segment, let us look again at the nature of what the Christian church calls "original sin" – Adam's sin.

God creates Eden and in this paradise he places various creatures, among them a man and a woman. The humans differ from the animals in that they have been invested with the ability to reason – to deliberate and to make choices. Despite this, however, the man is forbidden on pain of eternal death to eat from a tree in the Garden of Eden because it bears "the fruit of the knowledge of good and evil."

But what could possibly be wrong in wanting to know the difference between good and evil? And why, if God didn't want Adam to know the difference between good and evil, did he give him the ability to reason? The distinguishing difference between men and animals is man's ability to weigh the various options in a given set of circumstances and make a rational decision. Moreover, if one doesn't know the difference between good and evil, how does one distinguish between what *is* good and what *is* evil? And beyond all this, why would God give Adam the power to choose when, being omniscient, he would know before doing so how Adam would react when tempted?

None of it makes sense.

The Actual Creation

Genesis, the first book of the Bible, begins with the words: "In the beginning God created the heavens and the earth."

Many, if not a majority of, adult Christians accept the Genesis account of the Creation of the universe as factual and many churches continue to teach it. They believe that at some distant time in the past God created the world and its first inhabitants over a period of six days, placing them in a pristine garden called Eden somewhere in the Middle East.

A seventeenth-century Roman Catholic bishop and Bible scholar, James Ussher, basing his calculations on the lifespan of the various descendants of Adam listed in the Genesis account, concluded that the Creation took place in the year 4004 B.C., and for many years churches taught this as Bible truth. A few still do.

It is, of course, nonsense. Fully formed human beings did not suddenly appear on the earth a few thousand years ago; humankind has evolved to its present state from subhuman progenitors who lived in Africa as long ago as 4.4 million years.

In 1974 some fossil remains of what would be named *Australopithecus afarensis* were discovered in Ethiopia by an expedition led by Dr. Donald Johanson, President of the Institute of Human Origins in Berkeley, California. He was able to determine that this tiny creature stood 1.07 metres tall but differed from other primates at that time in that she had a uniquely human feature, a knee joint that enabled her to walk upright. Concluding that the fossil remains were female, Johansen named her Lucy for the somewhat whimsical reason that while he was first examining the bones, the Beatles' song "Lucy in the Sky with Diamonds" was playing on his tape-recorder.

BETWEEN TWO AND THREE million years ago, an upright primate, *Australopithecus africanus*, emerged, and over a period of approximately one million years, developed a somewhat larger brain and more upright frame than his predecessors to become the progenitor of the species now called *Homo habilis*, the first tool-making creature. The crude stone tools and weapons that he fashioned and which have survived him gave him many advantages, not least the ability to scavenge from the kills of larger animals such as lions and other predators who frequented the African veldt and jungles at the time.

Homo habilis proved to be highly adaptable and survived as a species for some 500,000 years. His group evolved into a stronger, taller, and more intelligent hominid, with the brain capacity of a four-year-old child and not greatly different from *Homo erectus*, who emerged some two million years ago and began to spread through much of what is now Europe and – over a period as long as 120,000 years – as far as Asia.

To get a proper perspective on our predecessors and early human history, the reader should keep in mind that the universe has existed for billions of years and that our solar system (indeed, our galaxy) vast as it seems to us, is but an infinitely tiny part of the cosmos.

IN 1929, THE AMERICAN astronomer Edwin Hubble confirmed that, wherever we look, galaxies other than our own are moving away from us at incredible speeds. In the now familiar term, the universe is expanding.

Hubble theorized that, some ten to twenty billion years ago, when the entire universe was infinitesimally small and infinitely dense – not as large as the head of a pin – there was a cosmic beginning that has since been called the Big Bang, a split-second when that compressed matter exploded, breaking into multiplied billions of what, for convenience, we call celestial bodies, each hurtling away from the centre and from one another at incomprehensible speeds.

This debris formed galaxies, billions of them, each composed of stars, nebulae, globular clusters, and interstellar matter. Our galaxy, the Milky Way, is about 100,000 light-years in diameter (a light-year being the distance that light travels in one mean solar year, about 5,880,000,000,000 miles). You begin to grasp how vast this is when you consider that our sun in a mere eight *light-minutes* distant from the earth. Our solar system is about five billion years old and our sun is not an exceptional star in the Milky Way galaxy. The star nearest earth is Proxima Centauri and it is about four light-years distant. Restated more simply: *light from the nearest star in the universe – travelling at 186,000 miles per second – takes four years to reach us!*

THERE ARE IN THE universe one hundred billion galaxies, each containing some one hundred million stars. The observable universe is a million, million, million, million (1,000,000,000,000,000,000,000,000) miles across – and that doesn't include that part of the universe that is so far distant that the light from it hasn't reached us yet!

Moreover, the universe is not in stasis, it is expanding. Each galaxy is moving away from every other galaxy at different but incomprehensible speeds. The farther from the centre, the faster a galaxy is moving, and the distance between every galaxy and every component in every galaxy is increasing with every split-second.

All of which is beyond our understanding. The point is made here for no other reason than to emphasize that facts such as these make it patently impossible for a contemporary man or woman to accept the biblical explanation for the existence of our world. The Genesis accounts of the Creation, while interesting as early historical documents, are no more than the uninformed speculation of a relatively primitive people; a folk tale no more trustworthy than the bizarre imaginings of various other people around the world, all trying to make sense of their own existence.

Surely, the time is long overdue for those in the Christian church who continue to insist that the Bible is the infallible Word of God to abandon this outdated belief and to move into the realities of the twentieth century.

Man – the Creator

*M*an, not God, created the world – our modern world. According to the book of Genesis, Elohim created the world in six days and on the seventh day he rested. "And God saw everything that he had made, and behold it was very good."

Unfortunately, it wasn't.

God's plan for the world was a ticking time bomb, a scenario destined for disaster. Almost immediately the first man and first woman were disobedient; they ate of the forbidden fruit. The Creator, giving them no second chance, no opportunity to learn from experience, cursed them, their world, and their descendants, and cast them out of Eden.

Suddenly, these progenitors of all humankind were on their own in a world filled with pain, jeopardy, and death. Despite this, the first humans and their descendants increased in number and the most adaptable survived and multiplied. Across the centuries they developed skills and transformed their dangerous, hostile world to the point where a man with a superlative gift for expression would describe a part of it as "This blessed plot, this earth, this realm, this England." It was a case of men and women working to correct the horrendous problems they encountered and about which the Creator seems indifferent.

AS ANYONE WHO HAS travelled widely would agree, it *is* a wonderful world, and this despite the fact that there are droughts, famines, hurricanes, and earthquakes, and millions of men, women, and children ailing in mind or body or ridden by disease.

But if it is a pleasant place it has become so, in large part, through the endeavours of men and women, not the Creator. Across the centuries our planet has been changed almost beyond recognition through improvements in housing, transportation, medication, life expectancy, creature comforts, and convenience. Although it is far from being One World, and despite the fact that many parts of it are marked by poverty, sickness, and violence, it *is* a pleasant place.

The improvements were not, however, the result of interventions by the Creator; they are the product of the creativity, ingenuity, co-operation, and toil of humankind. Faced with the hostility and indifference of the universe, men and women moved to overcome the problems that plagued them. Recognizing the Creator's apparent unconcern, they committed themselves to solving the problems that beset them and have been able to allay much of the pain, poverty, and heartbreak that has bedevilled the world since time began.

It was the efforts of men and women, not a mythical god, that made this a better world.

Noah and the Great Flood

*A*nyone who wants to sustain the view that God is love would do well to avoid reading the story in the book of Genesis of Noah and the Great Flood, in which, exempting only the eight people of Noah's family and breeding pairs of all the animals permitted to board the ark, God drowns every man, woman, child, animal, and lesser creature on the face of the earth.

Although it is probably one of the half-dozen best-known stories in Western history, few Christians know the facts concerning it. The average churchgoer will tell you that God caused it to rain forty days and forty nights and that life on earth was preserved only because Noah built an ark and took aboard his family and two of every animal species on earth.

True in part, except that this synopsis bears little resemblance to the details of the biblical account.

YAHWEH, THE GOD OF Israel, has come to where he realizes that his initial blunder at the Creation has compounded to the point of universal lawlessness. Surveying the earth, "God saw that the wickedness of man was great in the earth," and that, "every imagination of the thoughts of his heart was only evil continuously. And it repented the Lord that he had made man on earth. And the Lord said, I will destroy man whom I have created from the face of the earth; both man and beast and the creeping thing, and the fowls of the air; for it repenteth me that I have made them."

He exempts one family, Noah's, "for Noah found grace in the eyes of the Lord." He informs Noah that he is going to precipitate a flood that will cover the entire earth and "destroy every living creature under heaven." Only he and his immediate family will be spared. He orders Noah to construct an ark and specifies the dimensions: 300 cubits long, 50 cubits wide and 30 cubits high (approximately 500 feet long, 85 feet wide and 50 feet high).* The ark is to be covered, inside and out, with pitch. The design specifies three decks, a single window and a door on one side.

Noah, his wife, and his sons, Shem, Ham, and Japheth, and their wives, are to go aboard. And, so that the original Creation will not be wasted, Noah is instructed to take with him "every living thing of all flesh; two of each sort," and to lay in stores: sufficient food for his family and the various creatures. Then, in what is clearly an interpolation into the original text, God changes his instructions. "Of every clean beast thou shalt take to thee by sevens, the male and his female. Of fowls of the air also by sevens . . . to keep seed alive upon all the face of the earth."

Later God reverts to the original number of two and informs Noah that he has seven days before the rains come.

THE DAY ARRIVES and into the ark they go: Noah and his family, the wild and domesticated animals, the birds, the snakes and other reptiles, all crawling creatures and "everything with wings" – including, presumably, the insects, they had to survive, too.

"And the Lord shut him in . . ."

The "windows of heaven opened, the springs of the great deep broke through" and it rained for 40 days and 40 nights. But that was not the end of it: the floodwaters continued to rise, and it was not until 150 days had passed that the ark came to rest on Mount Ararat – five months after the rains had begun!

---

* A Cubit was an ancient measuring system based on the length of a man's forearm from the elbow to the tip of the middle finger. It varied from 17 to 22 inches.

EVEN A CASUAL READING of the story will make it evident that it is not fact but a legend. So many and so obvious are the incongruities that the case against its validity as history hardly needs to be argued. Nevertheless, let us note some of them.

First: The building of the ark.

The impossibility of the undertaking is immediately evident when one realizes that the ark was built in the days before steel. There were no axes, no saws, no hammers, and no nails. Trees had be felled and fashioned into intersecting and adjoining planks with only the crudest of tools and made watertight with pitch.

Picture in your imagination four men and their wives trying to lay the keel of a ship as long as a football field, and then attaching to it the ribs and planking needed to build a seaworthy craft large enough and strong enough to house thousands of animals. Bear in mind that the ark was three decks high and would, of necessity, have to be partitioned into stalls and containment areas in order to protect the smaller creatures from the predators.

Naturalists have estimated that there were at the time approximately 40,000 varieties of mammalia, 1,600 reptilia, thousands of avian creatures, and approximately 700,000 insect species. How, pray, does one go about capturing two of each, confirm that they are male and female, transport and then house them in segregated enclosures? How does one round up such creatures as a pair of water buffalo, or two giraffes, or two crocodiles – or, indeed, two skunks? How does one capture and transport even one male rhinoceros – not to mention laying in the specialized food for each species – enough to last the five months they will be stabled in the ark? How does one family feed them daily, clean out their quarters, and dispose of the excrement – especially when there are only eight people to do it, and Noah and his wife are six hundred years old!

How, in seven days, could this tiny group construct this enormous ship, complete the worldwide roundup and get the various beasts, birds, reptiles, insects, and so on lined up at the gangplank ready for boarding? And how did the animals indigenous only to Australia or Brazil or the Americas, for instance, *get* to the Middle East? Presumably by swimming oceans, climbing mountains, crossing deserts, and making their way through jungles. Consider also the beasts native only to the Americas: the polar bear, the Arctic fox, the American bison, the grizzly bear . . .

And how, incidentally, do you check on the sex of two hippopotami? Or capture and transport a matched pair of Tasmanian devils, Indian cobras, American wolves, Bengal tigers, Florida alligators, Arctic seals, never mind the fleas, mites, gnats, hornets, dragonflies, and other insects, and get them all – *and* their specialized foods! – ready for boarding?

One's imagination pictures Shem and Ham checking an endless list and saying "Darn! We're short a lioness, a wildebeest, and a male cockroach. Go get 'em, Japheth. And while you're at it, bring in a pair of Cornish rock hens, the weasels just killed the ones we had . . . Wait a minute; I almost forgot – a supply of ripe carrion for the vultures."

THE INTERIOR OF THE ark would need to be a complex place. There would have to be separate living quarters for Noah's family of seven. Predators would have to be housed apart from their prey – one momentary lapse and the killing of any creature would mean the end of that species. Feeding time would have been demanding, not least feeding the animals with exotic diets, among them the koalas who eat only eucalyptus leaves and the pandas whose preference is bamboo shoots. And how do you feed a queen bee without a hive and worker bees? How do you feed a vampire bat? How do you feed those creatures that require fresh grain or fresh blood or fresh meat or fresh fish or other special foods to survive?

Think of the storage problems!

How do you lay in fresh meat for the carnivores when there is no refrigeration? Inasmuch as the ark was sealed for five months, the quantity of food required, whether meat or fish or grain or whatever, would be mountainous. Many animals eat their weight in food in weeks.

Some birds are seed-eaters, some are insectivorous, some carnivorous, some feed on the wing. If they were confined for five months, would their wing muscles not atrophy? And if they weren't confined but were allowed to fly about would there not be a considerable problem with the droppings?

Which raises the matter of ventilation. There was only one door (which God had shut) and one window – a hole in the hull . . .

I leave it to the reader's imagination.

And beyond all this there was the matter of light. The skies were overcast and the nights were black. Regardless, one had to do the chores, and these could not possibly be accomplished without the use of some form of burning torch or lamp. But would not the smoke foul the atmosphere? And, with so many occupants, would not the oxygen be depleted within days or weeks? Imagine conditions *by the end of the fifth month!*

THE READER SHOULD BEAR in mind that Noah and his live cargo were not in the ark a mere forty days. It rained for forty days, but the water kept mounting month after month until the entire earth was covered to a depth higher than the Himalayas, the highest point on earth.

Where did the water come from? The amount of water in the world is fixed. Atmospheric conditions draw water from the oceans, lakes, and rivers and return it in precipitation, but the total amount doesn't change. The Bible story suggests that the extra water came from "the springs of the great deep." Ancients believed that, inasmuch as they could dig into the ground and strike water for their wells, the interior of the earth was filled with water. It isn't. And even if it were, if enough water emerged from beneath the ground to cover the entire globe to a height more than five and a half miles high, the weight of it would collapse the surface of the earth.

THE FLOOD WATERS having subsided, the animals released, Noah and his family emerged from the ark to begin life over again. Yahweh gave Noah a sign – a rainbow in the sky, a promise never again to curse the earth – and he blessed Noah and his little family, telling them to be fruitful and multiply and replenish the earth.

However . . .

Not long afterward there were problems in the new paradise. Noah, now a farmer, planted a vineyard, got drunk, and passed out in his tent. Ham, the youngest of his three sons, "saw the nakedness of his father" and informed his brothers Shem and Japheth. They took a garment, and taking great care not to glimpse their father's genitals, backed into the tent and covered him. When Noah "awoke from his wine" and learned that Ham had seen him naked, he laid a curse, not on Ham but, for some reason, on Ham's son Canaan, condemning him to be "a servant of servants" to his brothers.

Noah lived for 350 years after the flood and, at the ripe old age of 950, he died.

IT IS OBVIOUS THAT the story of Noah and the Great Flood is no more than an ancient folk tale, an attempt by an unknown author (two separate authors, actually) to salvage something from the disaster of Eden. The first attempt at Creation had been bungled and had ended with Adam and Eve banished from the garden. Noah is to be the new progenitor, "a second Adam" from whom all humankind will proceed. Alas! – more bungling would follow.

The Testing of Abram

Abram, known to Jews as the Father of His People, follows in a direct line of succession from Adam through Noah's second son, Shem. He is one of the legendary figures of the Old Testament and is revered not only by Jews and Christians but also by Muslims, being their ancestor through Ishmael, the son of Hagar, an Arab. Muslims revere him and speak of him as Father of the Faithful and Friend of God.

One day, at the age of seventy-five, Abram made an astounding announcement. He said that Yahweh himself had told him to leave his father's house, and travel "unto a land that I will show thee. I will make of thee a great nation. I will bless thee and make thy name great; I will bless them that bless thee and curse him that curseth thee: and in thee shall all families of the earth be blessed."

So Abram took his wife, Sarai, his nephew Lot, with all their possessions, left his home in Mesopotamia, and in obedience to Yahweh journeyed to the border of Canaan. There, Yahweh appeared to Abram and said, "Unto thy seed will I give this land." Abram built an altar nearby and, after pledging his undying loyalty to Yahweh, continued on, heading south.

But there was "a famine in the land" so Abram continued on to Egypt.

Then, there occurred a sudden transformation in this man who claimed to have an intimate relationship with God. Approaching the Egyptian border, he said to his wife: "Thou art a fair woman to look upon. Therefore it shall come to pass, when the Egyptians shall see thee, they shall say, 'This is his wife' and they will kill me, but they will save thee alive. Say, I pray thee, thou art my sister: that it may be well with me for thy sake."

His prediction proved accurate: Pharaoh's sons met Sarai and reported her extraordinary beauty to their father. Subsequently, Pharaoh took her into the palace and made her one of his wives. As an expression of his gratitude, he made Abram a wealthy man. The text says, "And he entreated Abram well for her sake: and he had sheep, oxen, she-asses, he-asses, camels, menservants, and maidservants."

In that startling amorality frequently encountered in Old Testament stories, Yahweh, rather than punish Abram for his duplicity, "plagued Pharaoh and his house with great plagues." Pharaoh, learning the facts, summoned Abram and said to him, "What is this that thou hast done unto me? Why didst thou not tell me that she was thy wife?" Then, in an act of extraordinary magnanimity, he says, "Now therefore behold thy wife, take her and go thy way." And Pharaoh ". . . sent him away, and his wife, and all that he had."

So Abram left Egypt and travelled to Canaan, to the town of Bethel, a successful man "very rich in cattle, in silver, and in gold."

He prospered in Canaan but all was not well; he and Sarai had grown old and were childless. So Sarai went to Abram and told him, "Go in unto my maid, Hagar. It may be that I may obtain children by her." Hagar, an Egyptian, became pregnant and soon began to treat Sarai with contempt because she was not able to conceive. Sarai complained to Abram. His response? "Behold, thy maid is in thine hand; do to her as it pleaseth thee." Whereupon Sarai drove her maid from the house into the wilderness. There, one of Yahweh's angels comforted her, told her that she would have a son, Ishmael, and that Yahweh would so multiply her descendants "that they cannot be numbered."

Thus Abram became the progenitor of the Arab peoples.

A FASCINATING STORY, but little more than a legend of an ancient people. More important, it is an insight into the morality of the God of the Old Testament, which is quite astonishing by today's standards.

Look again at the essence of the story. Almighty God tells an eminent septuagenarian named Abram that he has momentous plans for him. Not least, he pledges to make him the father of a great nation, a people who will be as numberless as the sands of the sea. He then directs him to the border of Canaan, appears before him, and promises to deed the country to him and his descendants.

To put the story in perspective, try to imagine it happening today. Your morning paper reports that a prominent local citizen has been contacted by God on two occasions, during which the deity predicted the future, told him that he would become one of the great men in history, promised that he would be the founder of a new nation, and added that he and his fellow citizens would one day drive out the residents and take over a neighbouring country.

The man would be dismissed as a religious fanatic.

The problem when people talk to God is that only one party to the conversation is willing to reveal what was said and it is impossible to confirm that the discussion ever took place. Why then should a folk tale about God's revelation to Abram (or anyone else from Adam to Noah to Moses to Joshua, all the way down to the Bethlehem shepherds) be taken seriously? Conversations with the deity are not uncommon in the histories of ancient people because they are written after the great man is dead and lesser men feel it requisite to supplement reality with stories of miracles and supernatural interventions. These legends are taken as fact when written histories are finally inscribed.

Why, one might ask, if God spoke face to face with Moses, did he not talk to Napoleon, or George Washington, or John A. Macdonald, or Bismarck? Was not each of them "the father of his country," and did they not all cast a longer shadow than Abram?

If Abram were to hear the laudatory legends spun about him after his death he might well deny them, for shortly after his purported one-on-one conversations with Yahweh we see him involved in an act of venal and moral duplicity that would do credit to Machiavelli.

Knowing that powerful men in Egypt would lust after his beautiful wife, he got her to pass herself off as his sister. Not only would this protect him from harm, he thought, it might be financially advantageous. It was an astute judgement. Pharaoh, enchanted by Sarai, takes her into his court and demonstrates his appreciation by turning business opportunities Abram's way. There could be few acts of duplicity more reprehensible. Abram misrepresents himself and his wife, acts as a procurer for the Pharaoh, requires his wife to perjure herself and become a court prostitute, and benefits financially from the transaction!

After which Yahweh made a covenant with Abram in which he promised him a son, and his people the land of Canaan; this despite the fact that Canaan had been settled and occupied for generations by others.

The Escape from Egypt

*I*srael's escape from Egyptian slavery is a memorable story but one that yields internal evidence that it is an ancient Jewish legend and not credible as history.

The Israelites are held captive in Egypt and being worked as slaves. In a settlement at Midian, a town east of the Gulf of Aqaba, a man named Moses is hiding out from Egyptian justice. One day, tending a flock of sheep, he sees a nearby bush on fire. Oddly, it is not being consumed. As he draws closer for a better look, a voice emanates from the flames and the speaker identifies himself as Yahweh, "the God of Abram, Isaac, and Jacob." He tells Moses that he has seen the intolerable conditions in which his people are living and intends to deliver them from slavery and lead them to "a land in which the milk and honey flows."

Moses has not heard of Yahweh, but is finally persuaded to go before the reigning Pharaoh to seek permission to lead the Israelites into the desert for three days so that they may offer sacrifices to Yahweh – a transparent scheme to get them beyond Egyptian borders.

Moses is slow to agree, doubting his ability to convince the Egyptian court, so Yahweh arms him with three conjurer's tricks. If during his audience with Pharaoh he casts his shepherd's staff to the ground, Yahweh will turn it into a snake. Then, when he seizes it by the tail, it will be turned again into a rod. If he thrusts his hand into his robe and then shows it, it will be covered with leprosy. A second time and the leprosy will be gone. And, finally, if he takes water from the Nile and spills it on the ground, it will turn to blood.

Reluctantly – for he suffers from self-doubt and apparently has a speech impediment – Moses agrees to do as he is bidden on the condition that he be accompanied by his more personable brother, Aaron.

Moses delivers Yahweh's message. Pharaoh dismisses him out of hand. Moses then complains to Yahweh: "Pharaoh has never heard of you." Yahweh responds, "I will punish Pharaoh; you will see. He will be forced to set my people free."

Moses and Aaron now return to the court to reiterate their plea. Aaron throws down his staff and it turns into a snake. The court magicians duplicate the trick. Whereupon, in a bit of one-upmanship, Aaron's snake swallows the other snakes. But the magic is to no avail. Pharaoh refuses to let the Israelites go.

Yahweh now initiates a horrific sequence of plagues.

All the waters in Egypt, from the Nile to the water in every tub and vessel, are turned to blood. All the fish in all the lakes and streams die, creating a noxious stink. But, as Yahweh had predicted, Pharaoh is adamant.

The plagues continue:

- Frogs in the rivers, in the streets, in the palace, in the beds, in the kitchens; frogs everywhere.
- Millions of lice and then billions of tiny gnats.
- A plague that kills all the Egyptian livestock.
- Moses throws some soot into the air. It carries to all Egypt, and wherever it falls, on man or beast, they are covered with stinking, pustular boils.
- The worst hail and lightning storm in Egypt's history, killing every animal, flattening the crops, destroying the trees.
- A plague of locusts that devours all vegetation, infests every Egyptian home, even penetrates to the palace.
- Utter darkness for three days – except where the Israelites live.

Pharaoh finally makes a concession: "You may go," he says, "but your flocks and herds must remain." Moses refuses the offer.

Finally, the ultimate plague, a horror hardly to be imagined. At midnight, every first-born Egyptian child and every first-born animal will be destroyed. Yahweh will personally do the killing. He gives Moses detailed instructions on how to protect the Israelite families. They must slaughter a sheep or goat and smear some of its blood on the doorposts and lintel of the house. "When I see the blood," Yahweh says, "I will pass over you." Then, at midnight, Yahweh slaughters all the first-born children in Egypt: Pharaoh's eldest child, the first-born of the prisoner in his dungeon, and the first-born of all the cattle . . .

Now the Egyptians beg the Israelites to leave. Yahweh instructs Moses to tell the Israelites to demand of their Egyptian neighbours all their gold and silver adornments and their finest clothing, and so anxious are the Egyptians to have quit of them that they do as they are bidden. The text says: "Thus they despoiled the Egyptians."

And so it was that, after years of intolerable slavery, the Israelites marched out of Egypt – an estimated six hundred thousand men, plus women and children – carrying their possessions and driving their flocks and herds before them, and headed at last for the promised land.

WHAT AN ENTHRALLING story! I recall first hearing it as a child in Sunday school and being fascinated by it. But can the mature reader accept the tale as anything more than folklore? Do such things happen? Have they happened at any time in secular history? The story is but a lurid example of the kind of mythology that many tribes and nations developed about their origins and their forebears. The folk tales of many ancient peoples are replete with similar stories: wondrous tales of superhuman leaders, divine interventions, and miracles performed by their gods.

The troubling thing is that, because the story is in the Bible, millions of contemporary Jews and Christians close their eyes to the fact that it is a profoundly immoral story and reveals a cruel god.

Take an unbiased look.

Yahweh, who seems to have been indifferent to the suffering of his Chosen People during the years they have been enslaved in Egypt, suddenly turns up and wants to get involved. There follows a series of horrific plagues, climaxing in the murder of every first-born Egyptian child. The incredible part of the story is that these punishments were inflicted despite the fact that – as the text makes clear – Pharaoh *could* not assent to Moses' entreaties. He had no option: Yahweh himself had *made* Pharaoh adamant.

At the beginning of Chapter 10 Yahweh brags to Moses, "I have hardened [Pharaoh's] heart and the heart of his servants so that . . . one day thou mayest tell in the ear of thy son and of thy son's son what things I have wrought in Egypt . . . that ye may know that I am the Lord . . ." and how he made fools of the Egyptians. Again and again the phrase is repeated: Yahweh "hardened Pharaoh's heart, and he did not let the sons of Israel go."

Can one believe that a loving God, the Father of *all* humankind, could do such a despicable thing? It might be argued that punishing Pharaoh and his court was justified, but were there no individual Egyptian citizens for whom Yahweh felt compassion? Were there no decent men or women among them? Need their property, their live-stock, their farms and fields be destroyed? Did not the innocence of their first-born stir Yahweh's compassion as he went about slaughter-ing every last one of them? Was it necessary that every mother see her eldest child slain before her eyes?

Is this a God one might be expected to worship and to love? No, the Yahweh portrayed in the legend is clearly – as was common among ancient people – a vindictive and vainglorious tribal god and the story cannot possibly be taken as anything other than primitive folklore. It is clear in the text that Yahweh did these horrific things primarily to gain prestige among the various gods of that time.

For example, after the Israelites have left Egypt and are travelling through the wilderness, Yahweh concocts a devilish plan, its purpose to draw Pharaoh's troops into a pursuit and thus win glory for him-self. He directs the Israelites to turn back and make camp and to do so in a manner that will create the impression they have lost their way. "Pharaoh will think," Yahweh says (to paraphrase), " 'Look how the Israelites wander about; the wilderness has them confused.' Then I shall harden Pharaoh's heart and he will set out in pursuit of them.

I shall win glory for myself at the expense of Pharaoh and all his army. And the Egyptians will learn that I am Yahweh."

Yahweh drew Pharaoh into pursuit, planning a miraculous escape for the Israelites, an escape designed to achieve two things: to win Israel's loyalty and, not incidentally, to impress any gods who might be looking on. Yahweh would part the waters of the Red Sea, permit the Israelites to pass through on the sea-bottom, and when the Egyptian army followed, bring the waters crashing down.

The text reads: "The returning waters overwhelmed the chariots and the horsemen of Pharaoh's army which had followed the Israelites into the sea. And there remained not so much as one of them."

After which Moses was inspired to compose a hymn of praise. In part:

> I will sing unto the Lord for he hath triumphed gloriously.
> The horse and his rider hath he thrown into the sea . . .
> The depths have covered them:
> They sank into the bottom as a stone . . .
> Who is like unto thee, O Lord, among the gods? . . .
> The Lord shall reign for ever and ever.

But the horrific tale has not yet reached its conclusion. When Yahweh promised to deliver his people, he intended not merely to deliver them from the bondage of Egypt, but to lead them to Canaan, "a land where milk and honey flow" – this despite the fact that the land promised Israel had already been settled for generations by others.

"My angel will go before you," Yahweh says, and – to paraphrase – "I will lead you to where the Amorites, the Hittites, the Perizzites, the Canaanites, the Hivites and the Jebusites are. I will spread panic before you. I will make your enemies flee before you. *I will exterminate them!* But you must not bow down to their gods; you must destroy them utterly. You are to worship Yahweh, *your* God."

This from a God of love, the God who is "no respecter of persons," the God Christians, Jews, and all humankind are required to worship and praise.

The Ten Commandments

We come now to the Ten Commandments, the fundamental laws on which Judaism and Christianity are based. They are
the rules of conduct inscribed by God on tablets of stone and delivered through Moses to the Israelites.

Codified laws relating to worship and behaviour were not unique
to the Israelites. In prehistory, primitive families lived in isolation
from one another, their dwelling a cave or sheltered place, the members of each family fearful of and hostile to outsiders. The male head
of the family, because he was physically stronger and not essential to
the nurturing of the children, went out to hunt or gather food. The
female remained at home, giving birth, attending to the needs of the
young, and preparing food.

With the passage of time, individual families began to realize that
solitary living had disadvantages, that there were benefits to be gained
by joining with other families and forming a community. Not least,
there was safety in numbers. And by co-ordinating their activities, a
group of families could erect common buildings and more efficiently
round up and kill game. Problems, such as the removal of a large tree
fallen across a path in the forest, could be resolved, and raids by
marauding tribes could be repulsed.

From these and other experiences early man learned that co-
operation was useful and that there were benefits to be gained by
forming communities. Experience taught that if the community
was to persevere, the individual within the society had sometimes to

restrain his or her words and actions. To entrench the necessary modifications of behaviour, specific responsibilities and prohibitions were codified as laws. If, for instance, a man killed a neighbour, vengeance by members of the victim's family was inevitable – the response to violence had long been an eye for an eye, a tooth for a tooth. The reprisals would, however, often lead to escalating violence and sometimes to blood feuds. To avoid such threats to the solidarity of the community it became necessary to find a way to control anti-social acts. This led to the establishing of codes of acceptable behaviour, laws designed to achieve the peaceful settlement of disputes.

But such laws were mere covenants among people and needed for their validation a higher authority. So a wise Moses asserted that these and other laws be laid down as divine edicts. He carved his commandments on stone tablets and claimed that he had received them from the hand of Yahweh himself. And he reminded his people of their debt to the God who had "brought them out of the land of Egypt, out of the house of slavery."

They were eminently practical laws and reveal a touch of genius. If, for instance, a man murdered his neighbour, members of the victim's family would be almost certain to retaliate, matching or escalating the initial violence. Unless this chain reaction was stopped, no one's life would be safe and community would be impossible.

Thus the commandment, "Thou shalt not kill."

If a man stole from his neighbour, the victim would feel justified in stealing from him and soon no one's property would be secure.

Thus the commandment, "Thou shalt not steal."

If a man fornicated with his neighbour's wife, it could lead to bloodshed and be disruptive of order in the community. Moreover, parentage could be in doubt. Unless it was controlled, the stability of family life would be threatened.

Thus the commandment, "Thou shalt not commit adultery."

If a man lied about or maligned a fellow citizen, this could lead to strife, an increasing lack of trust, and the gradual disintegration of the society. Unless it was controlled, no one's reputation would be safe.

Thus the commandment, "Thou shalt not bear false witness against thy neighbour."

If a man showed his parents no respect and neglected them in their old age, the responsibility for their care would fall on the community. As well, the offender's own children might, in their turn, reject him. As a consequence, the family unit would be weakened, family life would disintegrate, and community solidarity would be jeopardized.

Thus the commandment, "Honour thy father and thy mother."

If a man was envious of his neighbour, or coveted his wife, his house, his servants, or his possessions, it could create rivalries, hatred, and violence. Unless it was controlled, the maintenance of peace and tranquillity would be impossible.

Thus the commandment, "Thou shalt not covet thy neighbour's house, his wife, his servants or his wealth."

THE BIBLE IS NOT AN easy read. It is studded with mind-numbing details concerning the lineage of the Israelites, the specifics of various covenants between Yahweh and his people, and the minutiae requisite for acceptable worship – everything from the kinds of foods to be eaten or avoided to the laws related to its preparation, to the specifications for building places of worship, to the preparation of and sacrifice of animals, to the proper observance of the Sabbath, and to the propriety and acceptability of clothing, food, sex, and daily duties – on and interminably on.

Yahweh is represented as requiring absolute and unquestioning obedience to every jot and tittle of his edicts, not infrequently on pain of death. He sought to govern every aspect of daily life. He is represented as personally ordering the design for the place of worship, the tabernacle, and, as well, the veil, the table, the ark, the altar for incense and the altar for burnt offerings, and the tools to be used during worship. He specified the amounts of gold, silver, and bronze to be used in the court. He even designed the robes for the high priest and the lesser priests.

When the Israelites had completed the tabernacle to his satisfaction, Yahweh turned to the sacrifices to be offered, and they were many. And bloody. Specific sacrifices were detailed to deal with the sins of the high priest and the lesser priests, the sins of the leaders of the community, the sins of the community as a whole, and the sins of individuals, whether deliberate or inadvertent.

In many cases the sacrifice required was an animal: a bull, a goat, a lamb, or, for those who could not afford such, a pair of turtledoves or pigeons. In each case, the animal's throat was slit and the blood poured at the foot of the altar. The animal was beheaded, skinned, and the legs removed. It was then eviscerated and the various parts, including the kidneys, bowels, and fat, burned in the flame. As Moses told his people, "The fragrance of the offering will be pleasing to God."

With the incredibly detailed list of sins likely to be committed, worship would have been a violent and bloody scene, difficult for the modern Christian to associate with the God he has been told to love and call "Father."

Why, one might ask, would a purportedly loving and compassionate God require such carnage as evidence of repentance and obedience? The reason was, of course, that at that time in history, Moses and Aaron saw it as necessary for the governing and perpetuation of the relatively vulnerable tribe of Israel in a hostile world and to help fashion their people into a cohesive whole.

THE GOD OF THE OLD TESTAMENT is utterly unlike the God believed in by most practising Christians. He is an all-too-human deity with the human failings, weaknesses, and passions of men – but on a grand scale. His justice is often, by modern standards, outrageous, and his prejudices are deep-seated and inflexible. He is biased, querulous, vindictive, and jealous of his prerogatives.

A careful rereading of the Old Testament only confirmed my doubts about the deity portrayed there. Wanting to believe, I found it impossible. The god revealed there is a primitive tribal god, created out of necessity to enable their leaders to mould a volatile and highly individualistic people into a cohesive group by uniting them about a central core of belief.

The Promised Land

*I*srael's escape from Egyptian slavery had come about through the direct intervention of Yahweh when he personally scourged the land with plagues, killed all the first-born, and drowned every last man in the Egyptian army. And now, having survived forty years of hardship in the wilderness, God's Chosen People come to the borders of Canaan, the fabled Promised Land.

A land "flowing with milk and honey" lies ahead. It will soon flow with blood.

WE HAVE BEEN TAUGHT from childhood that "God is no respecter of persons" and that he loves all humankind with an everlasting love. However, as we continue to examine the Old Testament record let the reader keep this question before him: Is this the God of whom the apostle Peter speaks, the God who is "longsuffering to usward, not willing that any should perish but that all should come to repentance," the God who is "no respecter of persons"? Or is he a blood-thirsty tribal god, prejudiced in his attitudes, boastful of his powers, jealous of his prerogatives and utterly indifferent to human suffering – except, of course, that of his Chosen People?

Hear the voice of Yahweh: "Behold: I am He and there is no God beside me. It is I who kills and makes alive. I wound and I heal. When I have whetted my glittering sword, I will take vengeance on my adversaries. I will make my arrows drunk with blood. My sword shall feed on flesh, on the blood of the wounded and the captives . . ."

This is the voice of a God of love?

AS THE ISRAELITES readied themselves for the campaign, Yahweh moved to strengthen their morale. To paraphrase: "You may say in your heart, 'These nations outnumber me; how shall I be able to dispossess them?' But do not fear them; Yahweh, your God, is among you – a great and terrible God. Your God will deliver them over to you and will harass them until they are destroyed. He will deliver their kings into your hand and you will blot out their names from under heaven. None will withstand you until you have destroyed them every one."

Later, celebrating the victory, the Psalmist will sing: "Happy be he who takes their little ones and dashes them against a rock. God will shatter the heads of his enemies so that you may bathe your feet in blood and the tongues of your dogs lap their share of the enemy."

THIS IS THE BIBLICAL account of the conquest of Canaan. It is not a pleasant read. Canaan comprised an area at the eastern end of the Mediterranean, the land familiarly known as Palestine. It is now occupied in large part by Syria, Lebanon, Jordan, and modern Israel.

We now go back in the Bible to the time shortly after Moses has died and Joshua is in command of an army of forty thousand men. For forty years the Israelites have wandered in the wilderness and struggled to stay alive. Now, the journey ended, they are encamped on the near bank of the Jordan River.

The two men sent on ahead to spy out the land return, jubilant with excitement: Yahweh has delivered the whole country into our hands! they cry. Already the inhabitants tremble at the thought of us.

But first, the Jordan must be forded, and Yahweh is ready with the requisite miracle. Twelve men, each representative of one of the tribes of Israel, raise and carry the Ark of the Covenant to the bank of the river. The moment the feet of the bearers step from the bank, the waters cease their flow and flood the land upstream. Downstream, the river bed is exposed, and all Israel crosses dry-shod until the whole nation had finished crossing the river.

But before the invasion begins Yahweh insists that essential matters be taken care of. All the men who had come out of Egypt and were old enough to bear arms had died during the years in the wilderness. But none of the younger men who replaced them had been circumcised, and Yahweh has sworn not to let them see the Promised Land until they are.

Yahweh said to Joshua, "Make knives of flint and circumcise the Israelites again." And Joshua made knives of flint and circumcised the Israelites on the Hill of Foreskins. Then, "when the circumcising of the whole nation was finished, they rested in the camp until they were well again."

NOW TO THE CONQUEST of the Promised Land.

Jericho is the first city to fall. For six consecutive days the Israelites march in an eerie silence around the walled city Then, on the seventh day, as the seven priests leading the march blow on ram's horns and the people let out a great shout, the walls of the city fall down. The assault is made and the city is taken. "Then," as the record states, "with the edge of the sword, they utterly destroyed everyone in the city: men and women, young and old, oxen, sheep, and asses," and later burned it to the ground.

The next objective is the city of Ai. The first attempt fails. The reason? Yahweh is not with them. Earlier he had issued a ban: All the silver and all the gold, everything of bronze or made of iron is consecrated to Yahweh and must be put into his treasury. But one of the soldiers took for himself a fine robe, two hundred silver shekels, and an ingot of gold. When he confessed his crime, "All Israel stoned him," and Yahweh ceased from his burning anger.

Now Joshua and his men return to Ai. In a battle outside the walls, they kill every fighting man. Afterwards "all Israel entered the city and slaughtered all its people. The number of those who fell that day – men and women together – was twelve thousand, all the people of Ai."

There was a temporary setback when the king of Jerusalem formed an alliance with five other kings and occupied the city of Gibeon, which the Israelites had taken earlier but had not destroyed. Joshua and his army made a forced march through the night and caught the enemy unawares, whereupon Yahweh personally took a hand in the fighting. He drove the enemy from city to city "and hurled huge hailstones from heaven which killed them. More of them died under the hailstones" the record says, "than by the edge of Israel's sword."

But night was approaching and there was concern that some of the enemy might escape under cover of darkness. So Joshua stood and declaimed:

> Sun! Stand still at Gibeon.
> Moon! Stay over the valley of Aijalon.
> And the sun stood still and the moon stayed
> Until the people took vengeance on their enemies.

The story continues: Is it not written in the book of Jashar? The sun stood still in the middle of the sky and delayed its setting for almost an entire day. There has never been a day like it, before or since, a day in which Yahweh obeyed the voice of a man – for Yahweh was fighting for Israel.

On to Makkedah, which Yahweh delivered into the power of Israel, and Israel "struck every living creature there with the edge of the sword and left none alive."

To Libnah, "where Israel struck every living creature with the edge of the sword."

To Lachish, "which Israel took on the second day and struck every living creature with the edge of the sword and left none alive."

To Horam, whose king had dared to try to help the people of Lachish: "There Joshua struck him and his people down until not one was left alive."

To Eglon, where the Israelites were victorious again and "every living creature" slaughtered.

To Hebron, "where he left not a man alive."

And finally to Debir, where they "took it, and smote it with the edge of the sword, and its king and its towns, and every person in it; he left none remaining."

The record of the battles in southern Canaan is summarized thus:

"And Joshua conquered them from Kadesh-barnea to Gaza, and the entire region of Goshen as far as Gibeon." All these kings and their kingdoms Joshua mastered in one campaign because Yahweh, the God of Israel, fought for Israel!

BUT THE CONQUEST OF the Promised Land was not yet over. A coalition of northern kings now moved against Israel. "They set out with all their troops, a horde as countless as the sands of the sea, with innumerable horses and chariots."

But Yahweh said to Joshua. "Do not fear these men. By this time tomorrow you will see them cut to pieces. All of them! Then you will hamstring their horses and burn their chariots."

The following day, Yahweh delivered them into the power of Israel. Joshua harried them until there was not one left to escape. Whereupon, as Yahweh had ordered, he "hamstrung their horses and burned their chariots."

JOSHUA AND HIS ARMY now returned to Hazor, putting its king and every living creature there to the sword. Not a soul was left alive and Hazor was burned to the ground. He then captured the remainder of the royal cities but did not burn them, taking as spoils all the valuables and the cattle. "But they struck all the human beings with the edge of the sword and wiped them all out – men, women, children – they did not leave a living soul."

There was a clean-up operation – from Mount Halak to the valley below Mount Hermon – during which Joshua "captured their kings and slaughtered them all." The saga then concludes with an astonishing statement: Yahweh "had ordained that the hearts of these men should be stubborn enough to fight against Israel . . . so that they might mercilessly be exterminated. [Italics mine]"

In all, thirty-one kings were killed, as were their subjects: all of the men, most of the women, and many of the children.

"Then," the text concludes, "the country had rest from war."

IS THERE IN HISTORY a bloodier tale? Who can begin to measure the horror? The hand-to-hand fighting of that time was horrible. Few were killed with a single slash of the sword or thrust of the spear. Death often did not come quickly, as it so often does in modern war with the deadly impact of bullets and shells and bombs. And after each battle there would be hundreds of wounded to be dispatched.

The order from Yahweh was that none were to be left alive.

Can the reader believe for a moment that, if there is a God, he is like this?

The Patience of Job

*T*he Book of Job is one of the world's literary masterpieces. It is, however, neither fiction nor fact. It is an attempt by an anonymous writer (the date unknown) to explain in a biblical context the apparent paradox of undeserved suffering.

Job had observed that neither good fortune nor undue suffering seemed to have any consistent relationship with either the character of the individual or the justice of God. He voices the question that everyone has asked at some point in life: Why do the wicked so often prosper? And why, if there is a loving and just God, do so many good and caring people suffer ill fortune, sickness, sorrow and pain?

It is evident, on the face of it, that the Book of Job is not history but a fable. Job represents what is best in humankind. He is the embodiment of the decent and intelligent man.

It is possible that, in his zeal, the author of the Book of Job may not have realized that the God he portrays is a cruel and callous despot. The reader will clearly see that Job is more moral and compassionate than God. Indeed, Job's God is an unfeeling tyrant who, in order to win an argument with his adversary, Satan, permits Satan to inflict on God's paragon, Job, every personal, physical, and financial misfortune that could possibly befall an individual.

In brief compass and in contemporary language, this is the story:

ONE DAY THE "sons of God" come to attend on Yahweh. Among them is Satan.

"Where have you been lately?" Yahweh asks him.

"Going to and fro on the earth," Satan responds. "Observing."

"Did you take note of my servant Job?" Yahweh asks. "There is no one like him, an honourable and honest man who fears Yahweh and shuns evil."

"True," Satan replies. "But Job is not God-fearing for nothing. You have protected him and his family and have made him wealthy. But lay a finger on his possessions and he will curse you to your face."

"Very well," Yahweh says. "He is in your hands. Do with him as you please, but with one provision. You may not do him physical harm."

All hell breaks loose. A Sabean tribe raids Job's land and carries off five hundred yoke of oxen and five hundred donkeys. Lightning kindles a fire that destroys his seven thousand sheep and their shepherds. An enemy steals his three thousand camels and kills all his servants save one. Then, the final blow. A report comes to him: "Your sons and daughters were having a party when a gale destroyed the house and killed them all."

Job mourns his losses but nonetheless says:

Naked I came from my mother's womb;
Naked I shall return.
Yahweh gave,
Yahweh has taken away;
Blessed be the name of Yahweh.

Again the "sons of God" come to attend on Yahweh. Among them is Satan.

"Where have you been lately?" Yahweh asks him.

"Going to and fro on the earth," Satan responds. "Observing."

"Did you notice my servant Job?" Yahweh asks. "There is no one like him: a blameless and honourable man who fears God and shuns evil. You provoked me to ruin him but he remains faithful."

"Of course he does," Satan says. "But you didn't lay a hand on Job himself. A man will forfeit anything so long as he has his health. But afflict his body and he will curse you to your face."

"Very well," Yahweh says. "Do what you will. But you may not take his life."

So Satan afflicts Job with malignant ulcers, from the soles of his feet to the top of his head. Vermin infest his flesh, which becomes covered with loathsome scabs and oozing pus. Such is his torment that he takes to sitting in a garbage dump, scratching his itching sores with the shards of a broken pot.

His wife comes to him and says, "Why don't you curse God and die?"

Three of his friends – "Job's comforters" as they have come to be called – visit him in his afflictions. They are Eliphaz, Bildad, and Zophar. So stricken is Job that, at the sight of him, they rip their garments and throw dust on their heads. They insist that, despite Job's apparently blameless life, there must be a reason for the fate that has befallen him. They continue their accusations with Job insisting on his innocence.

At long last they leave off and another friend, Elihu, joins them. He is infuriated that Job continues to insist that he is right in his protestations of innocence, thus putting God in the wrong. And he is angry that Job's three friends have given up the argument, thus leaving the inference that God is unjust.

"How can you continue to insist that your suffering is undeserved?" he asks Job, and then goes on to lecture him and his friends, arguing that God's goodness is sometimes veiled.

Finally Yahweh himself turns up and, speaking from a whirlwind, establishes an all-time high in sarcasm: "What do *you* know?" he says to Job. "Where were *you* when I laid the foundations of the earth? Have *you* commanded the mornings? Have the gates of death been revealed to *you*? Tell me if you know: who has cleft a channel for the torrential rain and a passage for the thunderbolt? Tell me: has the rain a father? From whose womb did the ice come? Can *you* dispatch the lightnings that they may announce, 'Here we are'? Do *you* give the horse his strength? Is it by *your* wisdom that the hawk soars? . . ."

The tirade continues until, at long last, Yahweh says: "Does a faultfinder dare to contend with the Almighty? You! You who would argue with God . . . *Answer!*"

Job responds, "Behold, I am of little account; how can I answer God? I cover my mouth with my hand."

Whereupon God has at him again: "Have you an arm like God? Can you thunder with a voice like his, see the proud and abase him, tread on the wicked where they are? Who can stand before me? . . . You know nothing of how God works."

Then comes the clincher: "Do you *really* want me to reverse my judgement and thus put *me*, Yahweh, in the wrong and *you* in the right?"

Job yields. "I have been holding forth on matters I do not understand," he says. "But now, having seen you with my own eyes, I retract all I have said and in dust and ashes I repent."

Whereupon, Yahweh restores Job's fortune, doubling what it had been before. Subsequently, Job lives 140 years, fathers seven sons and three daughters, names the daughters Turtledove, Cassia, and Mascar, and, dies "an old man and full of days."

THE BOOK OF JOB IS such an extraordinary and engrossing fable and such a literary jewel that, apart from the author's intention, we may fail to hear what he is saying about the God whose case he is arguing. Reduce the story to its essence and this is what it says:

Yahweh makes a wager with his adversary, Satan, that Satan cannot shatter Job's faith. To back his assertion, he gives Satan a free hand to do his worst – without troubling to notify Job that he is to be the pawn in the game. To make his point, Yahweh has Job's livestock stolen, his servants murdered, his house burned, and his children killed in a fire. Then, for emphasis, he afflicts Job with a loathsome and agonizing disease. When, finally, Job does complain, Yahweh mounts a braggadocio defence and concludes by asking Job a pointed question: Is he willing to put Yahweh in the wrong in his wager with Satan so that he, Job, may be justified?

At this, Job repents of his complaining and Yahweh wins the wager. Job returns to a life of luxury and all's right with the world . . . although one cannot but ask: if God had killed *your* children simply to make a point in an argument, would the granting to you of other children make up for the horrible deaths and the loss of the first?

It is an immoral story and it portrays an immoral God. And it does nothing to answer the problem it sets out to deal with – namely, the problem of evil. Moreover, there was no need to do so; the biblical answer had already been given. In the Genesis story of the Creation we are told that suffering is God's punishment for sin. Because of the first man's disobedience in the garden, all his descendants must suffer sorrow, sickness, pain, and death.

Let the reader put the question: Is this the truth at the heart of life? And is it possible to believe this and continue to believe that "God is love"?

The God Men Created

Jesus of Nazareth

*I*t may come as something of a surprise to the reader to learn that we know remarkably little about Jesus of Nazareth. He died a young man in his early thirties, and the only records of his life that have survived are in the pages of the New Testament. But even these are second- or third-hand, and were written long after his death by men who never saw or heard him.

We don't know the date of his birth – it was certainly not December 25 in the Year One. Nor do we know for certain where he was born, although it was in all likelihood in the city of his childhood, Nazareth – certainly not in a Bethlehem stable. Nor do we know the exact date of his death, although it would seem to have been around the year 30 A.D. The great secular historians of that time (Tacitus, Josephus, Pliny the Younger, Suetonius, and others) mention Jesus only briefly, making passing reference to the fact that he preached in occupied Palestine and was crucified by the Roman government.

The earliest Christian records extant are the Pauline epistles, and they were written around 50 A.D. It was another ten years or so before the Gospels of Matthew, Mark, Luke, and John were completed. But the names attached to the gospels are pseudonyms – none of the authors were among Jesus' apostles and it is likely that none of them so much as saw or heard him.

LET ME TEMPER THESE negative assertions by making it clear that, while virtually none of the available information about Jesus is certifiable as historic fact, there can be no doubt that he did live, did enlist a group of disciples, preached through much of Palestine, said most of the things attributed to him, stirred widespread interest among the Jews of the area, kindled animosity – especially among the religious hierarchy – was arrested by Roman soldiers and was, after a brief and farcical trial, cruelly put to death by crucifixion on a Roman cross.

It has been suggested that Jesus went to his death not absolutely sure himself who he was. The despairing cry on the cross, "My God! My God! Why hast *thou* forsaken me?" seems to suggest that in the final hour of his agony – his enemies triumphant, his Father in Heaven having dispatched no "legion of angels" to effect his rescue – he came to doubt himself and his mission. He had been forsaken by the crowds who had earlier flocked to hear him and they had been replaced by his enemies: the religious leaders, the idlers, the curious and the passersby who mocked him as he struggled in the death agony. Even his closest friends had turned craven and fled into hiding. Judas, the treasurer of his little band, had betrayed him and then committed suicide.

Examining such data as is available, it is not possible to believe that Jesus was resurrected. Apart from the Gospels there is no evidence that he was. And a careful examination of the Gospel accounts makes it evident that they are mutually contradictory, lack authenticity, and are in large part of the nature of legends.

The stories of Jesus' entry into Jerusalem, his cleansing of the Temple, and his arrest, trial, and crucifixion have about them an aura of reality but, beyond that, the various accounts differ so radically and at so many points that, with all the good will in the world, they cannot be reconciled.

The Temptation in
the Wilderness

What is one to make of the story of Jesus' temptation in the wilderness?

Even a perfunctory reading makes it clear that the story is little more than a folk tale and is unworthy of inclusion in the canon of the Scriptures. It is recounted in three somewhat differing versions in Matthew, Mark, and Luke and is an attempt to demonstrate Jesus' identification with mankind and the magnitude of his commitment.

Immediately following his baptism in the Jordan, Jesus is portrayed as being led by the Holy Spirit into the wilderness "to be tempted by the devil. He fasted forty days and forty nights and afterwards he was famished."

The Devil – described in Matthew's version as "the Tempter" – comes to him and says, "If you are the Son of God, command these stones to become loaves of bread." Jesus answers him, saying: "One does not live by bread alone but by every word that comes from the mouth of God."

Then the Devil took him to the holy city and placed him down on the pinnacle of the temple, saying to him, "If you are the Son of God, throw yourself down: for it is written, 'He will command his angels concerning you'; and 'On their hands they will bear you up, so that you may not dash your foot against a stone.'" Jesus responds by saying: "Again it is written, 'Do not put the Lord your God to the test.'"

The Devil now takes him to the top of a very high mountain and

shows him all the kingdoms of the world and their splendour. "All
these I will give you if you will fall down and worship me."

Jesus said to him, "Away with you, Satan! for it is written,
'Worship the lord your God, and serve only him.'"

The tale concludes with the Devil departing. "And suddenly,
angels came and waited on him."

THAT THE STORY IS A fable is obvious. Its purpose is to emphasize
the human side of Jesus. The author (unknown) is clearly trying to
impress on the reader Jesus' humanity and the depth of his commitment by demonstrating that, as all men are, Jesus was subject to temptation and therefore capable of sin. If not, what is the point? And,
being a man, Jesus could have sinned, of course. And if he had sinned
would not the Father – being "no respecter of persons" – have to deal
with him as he dealt with Adam – banishing him from his presence?
Moreover, if Jesus could have yielded to temptation, does it not follow that God the Father could, too? Are they not one?

The story is ill-conceived and quickly collapses under the weight
of its own contradictions.

The Birth of Jesus

No part of the Christian story is as familiar as the events surrounding Jesus' birth. Is there a child in Christendom who cannot recount the essential details in the Gospels? Christmas, Good Friday, and Easter – the high holy days of the Christian church – and yet all three are replete with irreconcilable contradictions and not credible as history.

CHRISTMAS!

"It Came upon a Midnight Clear." "O Come All Ye Faithful." "Joy to the World, the Lord Is Come." A very pregnant young woman on the back of a donkey on the long journey from Nazareth to Bethlehem. Her husband, the bridle in his hand, trudging by her side. No room at the inn. Shelter in a stable. Cattle lowing in the nearby stalls. The birth of the babe. The angelic announcement to the shepherds watching their flocks by night. The star in the night sky leading the Wise Men to the stable. The presentation of their gifts of gold, frankincense, and myrrh. The slaughter of the infants by Herod's soldiers. The flight into Egypt to escape the murderous king . . .

Is there in the Western world a more familiar and more treasured story? One hesitates, therefore, to point out that it is no more than a fable and certainly not history. Once one opens one's mind to that possibility, the inconsistencies and contradictions of the biblical record – and beyond that, secular history – make this clear.

BEGIN WITH THE STAR of Bethlehem.

Can a contemporary man or woman believe for a moment that an astral body could actually "go before the Wise Men until it came to rest over the place where the child was"? The story was credible in biblical times when stars were thought to be mere lights in the nearby vault of the heavens and not, as we now know, luminous planetary bodies, blazing suns, or distant galaxies, millions of miles distant.

I will not attempt to detail here the cataclysmic events that would have resulted had such a phenomenon happened: enough to say that it would have left the Bethlehem area destroyed. And surely if such an extraordinary celestial event had taken place it would be mentioned somewhere in the history of at least one of the peoples of that era. There is, however, no such record.

LET US EXAMINE THE essentials in Matthew's and Luke's accounts of Jesus' birth, noting how fundamentally they differ.

In Matthew's account, Joseph and Mary live in Nazareth and are engaged to be married. Prior to the marriage, Joseph learns that Mary is pregnant. Being a decent man, he is not willing to make a public example of her but is of a mind to break off the engagement. An angel appears to him in a dream saying " 'Fear not to take unto thee Mary thy wife, for that which is conceived in her is of the Holy Ghost. When she is delivered of the child you are to name him Jesus [Saviour] for it is he who will save his people from their sins. The infant is to be the fulfilment of a biblical prophecy: 'Behold a virgin shall conceive and bear a son. And they shall call his name Emmanuel – God with us.' "

Some astrologers ("wise men from the East") arrive in Jerusalem, seeking information about a "King of the Jews" who, according to prophecy, was to be born in the town of Bethlehem. They are questioned by King Herod and ordered to bring him word of the infant's whereabouts when they find him. Following the star, they find Jesus' family in Bethlehem, not in a stable but in a house, and there they present their gifts of gold, frankincense and myrrh. Warned in a dream not to return to Herod, they press on to their homes by another route.

Later, an angel appears to Joseph in another dream and tells him that Herod has instituted a search to find the infant and kill him. The angel instructs Joseph not to return home but to flee to Egypt until the danger has passed.

Following Herod's death in 4 B.C. Joseph has yet another dream. In it he is informed that the danger has passed and that he and his wife and infant son may now return to Palestine. They set out for home, but learning that Herod has been succeeded by his son, Archelaus, go instead to Nazareth.

In Luke's account, the infant Jesus is circumcised in the Temple in Jerusalem eight days after his birth. On the fortieth day he is with his parents in Jerusalem when Mary undergoes the mandatory Jewish rite of purification, after which the family returns to their home in Nazareth.

But Matthew's account makes this impossible. When, according to Luke, Jesus' circumcision and Mary's purification were taking place in Jerusalem, Matthew asserts that the Holy Family was hiding out in Egypt awaiting the death of Herod, and it is not until after Herod's death that they return to Palestine and begin life in Nazareth.

Earlier Matthew states: "Then Herod, when he saw that he had been tricked by the wise men, was in a furious rage." He dispatched soldiers to kill every male child in Bethlehem and the outlying region who was two years old or younger, "according to the time which he had ascertained from the wise men." There is, however, nothing in the records of Herod's reign – or in the histories of any other people at that time – that makes any reference to what would surely have been a bloody and unforgettable slaughter.

The fact is the two accounts cannot be reconciled. It seems likely that the birth in Bethlehem was inserted into the story at a later date to validate the claims made by Jesus' followers that, through Joseph, he stood in a direct line of descent from King David, whose roots *were* in Bethlehem. It should also be noted that neither of the other Gospels, Mark or John, makes any reference, direct or indirect, to any of the above events. One would expect that they would, inasmuch as they were written by men who would have wanted to include in their accounts of Jesus' life any extraordinary events related to his birth, particularly because such stories would help validate the claims that Jesus' birth fulfilled various Old Testament prophecies.

ALL THE FOREGOING leads us to the teaching of the Christian church that Jesus was born of a virgin. It is not surprising that claims were made that Jesus' birth was miraculous. The birth of many of the gods in history have given rise to extraordinary legends. The Christian church has always insisted that Jesus' mother, Mary, was impregnated not by her husband but by God himself in the persona of the Third Person of the Holy Trinity, the Holy Ghost. The Roman Catholic church goes even farther, proclaiming not only that Mary was a virgin when Jesus was conceived but that she remained a virgin throughout her life.

Let us examine the record; rendering the text in contemporary English: In the town of Nazareth, in the province of Galilee, there lived a woman by the name of Mary, a virgin. She was engaged to be married to a carpenter by the name of Joseph, a direct descendant of David, the one-time King of Israel.

God sent the angel Gabriel to Mary: "Greetings, favoured one," the angel said. "The Lord is with you."

Mary was much perplexed by his words and pondered what kind of greeting this might be. "Do not be afraid," the angel said to her, "for you have found favour with God. And now you will conceive in your womb and bear a son, and you will name him Jesus. He will be a great man and will be called the Son of the Most High. And the Lord God will give him the throne of his ancestor David . . . and of his kingdom there will be no end."

"But how can that be?" Mary said. "I am a virgin."

"The Holy Spirit will come upon you," the angel said. "And the power of the Most High will overshadow you; therefore, the child to be born will be God's holy son. He will be called the Son of God."

"Here am I," Mary said, "the servant of the Lord; let it be according to your word."

Prior to the wedding Joseph learned that Mary was pregnant. He was a decent man, and not wanting to see her disgraced, planned to break off their engagement quietly. But while he was pondering what course to take, he had a dream in which an angel spoke to him.

"Joseph," the angel said, "do not be afraid to take Mary as your wife. The child conceived in her is from the Holy Spirit. She will bear a son, and you are to name him Jesus, for he will save his people from their sins."

The Roman Catholic church has gone far beyond merely asserting Mary's lifetime virginity. In 1854 it proclaimed that Mary was *herself* conceived without original sin, led an immaculate life, and was "assumed" into heaven, not knowing the fate common to all mortals, death. Mary has since been officially designated an object of veneration by Catholics – veneration as distinct from worship. Despite this, prayers are offered to her daily and her favours are sought. It has been argued by some popes (although there is not one word in the Gospels to validate it) that Mary's suffering at Calvary was so great that she is in fact "co-redemptress," actively participating with her son in the salvation of humankind.

It is not difficult to understand the increasing emphasis on Mary by the Roman church. The Old Testament and the New – and, indeed, the Roman church itself – are male-dominated and there is a growing negative reaction by women to this imbalance.

The Christian church's traditional insistence that Jesus was God, the Second Person of the Holy Trinity, and that his mother was a young unmarried Jewish virgin who was impregnated by the Holy Ghost, is incredible. If one approaches the New Testament account with an open mind and unflinching realism, the evidence clearly indicates that Jesus was an illegitimate child who, when he came to maturity, resented it and was alienated from his parents and siblings.

Jesus' Alienation
from His Family

*I*f one is to begin to understand Jesus of Nazareth, it is essential to examine not only what he said and did in his public ministry, but also something of his family life, his relationships with his parents and siblings. And here, our only sources of information are the narrative portions of the Gospels and what Jesus himself had to say on the subject of home, parents, and family.

Again, let us examine the record in the Gospels.

While preparing to begin his public ministry – having already chosen five of his disciples – Jesus was a guest at a wedding in Cana in Galilee. His mother was there, too. She came to him and told him that there was something of a crisis – their host had run out of wine. Jesus responded with what, on the face of it, can only be described as rudeness. "Woman," he said, "what concern is that to you and to me? My hour has not yet come." Nonetheless, the story continues, he averted his host's embarrassment by turning some of his well-water into the finest of wine.

There may have been some unstated reason why Jesus spoke to his mother so rudely but his response seems, in any circumstance, anything but filial and loving. He not only does not call her Mother – but "woman" – he virtually disowns her, saying: "What do you have to do with me?"

This apparent alienation seems further evident when, early in his ministry, having begun to attract widespread attention, Jesus returns to his home town, Nazareth, for a visit and goes to dinner at a neighbour's home. Mark's Gospel reports that, "A crowd gathered, so large that they could not so much as eat." Some of those present reacted to what Jesus was saying with such comments as: "The man is beside himself." and "He is possessed by Beelzebub" (the Devil).

His family, hearing about this, went to the house, and remaining outside, "called to him" and "sent word to him." Someone brought the message to Jesus: "Your mother and your brothers are outside and asking for you." Jesus responded by, it would seem, disowning his family. Looking around at those about him, he said, "*These* are my mother and my brothers. Whoever does the will of God is my brother and sister and mother."

It may be argued that he was simply using the incident to make a point, but let the reader ask: would he or she – in *any* circumstance – so cruelly dismiss in public his mother and siblings?

THIS WAS FOLLOWED BY another somewhat similar incident. Jesus has been teaching elsewhere. He returns to Nazareth and is preaching in the synagogue. His neighbours and the townsfolk are impressed but puzzled. They say to each other (to paraphrase): "Where did this man get all this? Is this not the carpenter? Isn't his mother, Mary? Aren't James and Joseph and Simon and Judas his brothers, and are not his sisters among us? Where does he get all this?"

As the text says, "And they took offence at him."

Jesus' immediate response is understandable. A prophet, he says, is not without honour except in their home town and among their own kin.

The apparent bitterness in his words more than suggests that he was alienated from his mother and siblings.

This alienation is further evident in some references to home and family in Matthew's Gospel. Early in his itinerant ministry Jesus and his disciples are walking down a road in Palestine. He notices a man standing nearby and calls out to him, "Come. Follow me." The man's father having just died his response seems entirely reasonable: "Lord, let me first go and bury my father." But again Jesus' response suggests a low opinion of family relationships: it is, to say the least, insensitive and lacking in compassion: "Follow me, and let the dead bury their own dead," he tells the man. "You go and proclaim the Kingdom of God."

Another potential recruit calls out, "I'm prepared to follow you, sir, but let me first go and say goodbye to my family." Again Jesus' response seems unfeeling: "No one who puts a hand to the plough and turns back is fit for the Kingdom of God."

On yet another public occasion he makes an even more astonishing statement. He says, "Whoever comes to me and doesn't hate father and mother, wife and children, brothers and sisters – even life itself – cannot be my disciple."

It seems clear in the above examples (and others) that, while the point being made speaks to the necessity for total commitment, Jesus felt little or no affection for – and, it would seem, considerable animosity toward – his family.

The textual evidence portrays a man alienated from his family.

What could have been the reason? Might it not be that he knew he was a child born out of wedlock (a so-called illegitimate child) and learning of it in his childhood and perhaps being taunted about it by his siblings or playmates or by some caustic adult – "Mary's little bastard" – would have come to resent his mother and the circumstance of his birth? In a small town, where everyone knows everyone else's business, his parents' untimely marriage would not have escaped notice; especially when, as the text points out, Mary left town and went off to Bethlehem for the birth of the child. It seems evident that they had no relatives or friends in Bethlehem. If they did, why did Mary apparently have no option but to give birth in a stable?

AS JESUS CAME TO maturity he appears to have entirely rejected his family. Early on, he left his home in Nazareth and made Capernaum his base. His mother disappears entirely from the record, as does his father, and she is not so much as mentioned again until his crucifixion, where – in a reference, the authenticity of which is questioned by textual scholars – she is said to have been standing nearby with her sister and two others.

Jesus – the Man

What a disservice the Christian church has done to Jesus of Nazareth! He has been so misrepresented across the centuries that it is almost impossible for us to imagine him as he was. The church's greatest disservice? Turning this most uncommon of common men into a god.

Jesus is perhaps the single most influential man in the history of Western civilization. Even today, almost two thousand years after his death, the impress of his life and teaching is so profound that it touches each of us daily in some immediate or indirect way. Despite this, most of us know little about him, and what we do know has been altered by myth and coloured by misconception. In most of our representations of him – and they number in the thousands – he is portrayed as a hopelessly idealistic demi-deity, the Son of God, perhaps, but not *really* a man.

Anyone opening the pages of the New Testament expecting to encounter there the "gentle Jesus, meek and mild" of their Sunday-school days will be taken by surprise. Gentle he was; meek and mild he most certainly was not.

In the Gospels you find, unmistakably, a man: sweaty after effort, dirty after a journey on the dusty Palestinian roads. He felt fatigue, was often impatient, sometimes rude, and on more than one occasion, enraged. "The Prince of Peace"? Not Jesus of Nazareth. He said of himself, "Do not think that I have come to bring peace on earth, but a sword." His ministry was passionate with conflict and noisy with

97

controversy. Those who heard him loved him or hated him. When he finished teaching, some were prepared to follow him anywhere; others were ready to form a lynch mob.

"Gentle Jesus, meek and mild"? He is more accurately described as a revolutionary. The charges that led to his being sentenced to death were that he challenged the system, taught heresy, and stirred sedition among the people.

Does that description fit the familiar marble figure standing expressionless in a niche in the sanctuary, hands extended so that you can see the scars on his palms and be moved to pity? Of course not. Jesus wasn't interested in anyone's pity. He wanted to change the status quo in the lives of individuals and in the society.

And not some distant someday down the road: *Right here! Right now!*

IN ORDER TO COMPREHEND Jesus' greatness it is necessary to remove the halo from his brow. To continue to insist that this unique human being was Almighty God disguised as a man is to make him unlike us and to deprive ourselves of the benefits to be derived by taking seriously what he said, the unique way he lived, and the manner in which he died.

Recognizing him as human we can identify with him, learn from him, measure ourselves against his teachings, and strive to follow his example. Surely at this point in history it is time to have done with theological obfuscation and priestly maunderings on the subject of his divinity. They are as outdated as is the medieval nonsense once taught by the church that the earth was the centre of the universe and that the sun and planets revolved around it.

If Jesus had known that following his death he would be resurrected and returned to heaven, then his dying – for all the agonies of the crucifixion – would not have been the utter horror that it was. If he was on the eve of a return to his Father and his heavenly home, why the enormity of his agony in the Garden of Gethsemane where, according to Luke's Gospel, he pleaded with the Father to be released from his mission, "sweating, as it were, great drops of blood" and crying out, "If it be possible, let this cup pass from me"? Many were crucified by the Romans in that era and if Jesus really was God in human flesh and knew the end from the beginning, even crucifixion would not hold the horrors for him that it did for others who underwent a similar death.

In short: if Jesus was God in human flesh he was not like us and it is impossible to follow his example. If he was a man, he is a model, a challenge and an inspiration to each of us.

IT IS WORTH NOTING before concluding this segment that there is no mention of Jesus in the Old Testament, which, in the Christian context, does not make sense. If he was God, the Second Person of the Holy Trinity, co-equal, co-eternal, and co-existent with the Father, where was he and what was he doing during those centuries? We read about angels, about a rebellion in Heaven, about the banishing of Lucifer and the other rebellious angels, about the giants of Hebrew history and about God the Father's various teaching and activities, but not one word about a Jesus.

The reason is obvious: Jesus of Nazareth was *not* God, the Second Person of the Holy Trinity; he was a human being, born of male and female parents, who, on reaching maturity, became an itinerant preacher, gathered a band of twelve men as associates and travelled throughout Palestine preaching his flawed gospel of the coming Kingdom of God on earth. His closest followers, awed by his genius and his charismatic presence, concluded that he had to be more than a mere man. This is the reason for the fabrication of the story of the virgin birth and the reports about the miracles he is said to have performed. And it is the reason for the legend that he did not, as all men must, die.

The Messianic dream, having been born, could not be allowed to perish.

BUT HOW MUCH BETTER in our time to recognize for who he was this superlative human being, this wise, compassionate, and courageous man. It is easy to worship Jesus but it is difficult to live by his insights into the human condition and the human potential, and, within one's limits, to follow him.

Problems in
Understanding Jesus

Why is Jesus so little understood, so frequently misunderstood?

The principal reasons are the difficulties encountered when one sets out to learn about him. There was little, if anything, written about him during his lifetime, and there are only brief references to him by the secular historians of the time.

To begin to get the full story it is necessary to read all four Gospels. But there are conflicting reports and irreconcilable contradictions in what are called "the synoptic Gospels" (Matthew, Mark, and Luke), and the radically different style and intention of the author of the Gospel of John compounds the problem. Basic to that problem is that all the Gospels are second- or third-hand reports at best, written decades after Jesus' death by men who never saw him and had to depend on the most fragmentary writings or word-of-mouth accounts passed from generation to generation.

The author of the Gospel according to Matthew was an unknown Christian Jew, writing about 90 A.D. and living in the neighbourhood of Antioch in Syria. We know little about him except that he borrowed most of his data from what is now known as Mark's Gospel. Of the 661 verses in Mark, Matthew reproduces the essence of more than 600, often in language largely identical.

Another of his sources would seem to have been a narrative known to Bible scholars as Q, the Q signifying the German word

Quelle, "source." Q is the oldest "Gospel" known. It differs from the New Testament Gospels in that it is essentially a collection of the sayings of Jesus. It makes no reference to his birth, childhood, ministry, trial, or death.

The identity of the author of the Gospel of Mark is unknown. Mark is both the earliest of the four Gospels and the shortest. Internal evidence suggests that it was written after the Roman destruction of Jerusalem in 70 A.D. It has been argued that the author is the John Mark identified as a companion of the apostle Peter during Peter's stay in Rome, but this is now thought unlikely. Internal evidence also suggests that the final draft was written at Rome some time after Peter was martyred, during the persecution of Christians by the Emperor Nero in 64 A.D.

The author of the Gospel of Luke was not, as is commonly believed, the "beloved physician" referred to in Colossians, nor was he an eyewitness to the events he wrote about. This is made obvious by his statement that he bases his writings on "those things delivered to us by those who were eyewitnesses from the beginning." He borrows much from Mark and from Q, and even more from an unknown source known to Bible scholars as L. There is general agreement that the Gospel of Luke was written sometime between 80 and 90 A.D.,* decades after Jesus' death.

The Gospel according to John is unlike the others in style and, frequently, in substance. It is evident that the author did not set out to write a biographical account but rather a theological drama, and in doing this he sometimes employs a complex symbolism. He emphasizes his reliance on eyewitnesses and takes pains to cast the story in an historical form. There has been much debate about the date of John's Gospel; suffice it to say that it was written toward the end of the first century.

Such evidence as is available indicates that all four Gospels were composed generations after Jesus' death and were not immediately

---

* The author of Luke also wrote the Acts of the Apostles.

accepted by the early Church. Indeed, the first historian to make reference to all four was Iraneus, and he lived almost one hundred years after the Gospels were written.

It is assumed by most Christians that the Gospels are the earliest writings about Jesus, but they were preceded by the epistles of the apostle Paul. Most New Testament scholars agree that Paul's epistle to the Thessalonians is the earliest of all New Testament books. It was written around 62 A.D., probably just before Paul was executed by order of Nero.

Those who contend for the inerrancy of the Gospels assume a patently impossible task. Most Christians take it for granted that the original Gospels have come to us intact from New Testament times, but the oldest scrap of any of them is a tiny fragment of the Gospel of John, which has been dated at around 125 A.D. – almost a century after Jesus' death. It was not until the end of the second century that there were complete transcripts of the New Testament. None of the original manuscripts has survived.

Moreover, since all copies of the Gospels were handwritten prior to the invention of the printing press, which in the West was not until early in the fifteenth century, it is easy to understand why no two copies are identical. Bible scholars have estimated that there are as many as seventy thousand variations of consequence in the early texts of the complete New Testament.

Beyond all this, Jesus probably spoke Aramaic, and inasmuch as the early Gospels were written in Greek, it seems likely that Jesus' exact words have been irretrievably lost. This is not to suggest that the Gospels are not, essentially, trustworthy; oral teaching – which involved scrupulous memorization – was a carefully cultivated skill among Jews at the time. Nevertheless, in the early years, the Gospels were, in all probability, communicated by oral transmission and only later came to the written form.

The reader of the Gospels should know also that the books selected to be included in the New Testament were determined not by divine edict but by votes taken in various ecclesiastical councils, individual votes not infrequently being influenced by theological, rather than factual considerations.

There are other obstacles in reading the Bible that should be mentioned, not least the fact that it can be pretty heavy going. The most familiar translation, the King James Version, is archaic in style and language and is, for all its occasional literary beauty, often unintelligible to a modern man or woman. Moreover, the form in which the stories are presented – the frequently awkward segmenting of the narrative into numbered verses, for instance – is unfamiliar to a modern reader, often distracting and sometimes misleading. As a result, although the Bible has been and remains the unchallenged best-seller among English language books it is the least read. Most homes have a Bible but it is seldom opened. It is my considered judgement that not one in a hundred clergymen and not one in a thousand laymen has read the Bible from cover to cover. And little wonder: it is not an easy read and much of it is irrelevant in our time.

OBVIOUSLY, BELIEF IN the Gospels as the inerrant Word of God is impossible. This is not to suggest that the essentials of Jesus' life and teachings in the New Testament are not, by and large, accurate. Despite many inconsistencies and numerous contradictions, the Gospels present a vivid picture of an extraordinary man – a man beyond anyone's invention – whose words, actions, and attitudes mark him as one of the moral geniuses of history and as someone whose teachings have profound relevance today.

Jesus' Life

What can be said of Jesus of Nazareth with reasonable certainty? The fundamental fact about him, as Geza Vermes, a distinguished Jewish historian at Oxford University, has emphasized, is that he was a Palestinian Jew. Jesus was raised in Galilee and spent all of his youth and most of his adult life there. Galilee was a rural area, far removed from the relative sophistication of Jerusalem, a part of Palestine in which a primitive form of Judaism was practised. Jesus was born into a typical Jewish home, circumcised as all Jewish boys were, raised as a Jew, lived as a pious Jew would. He probably followed Judaic rituals more or less as his neighbours did and spoke Aramaic, the language of the common people.

Palestine was the heart of Jewish life after the Diaspora and was in Jesus' time a place of religious fervour and political dissent. As a young man Jesus would undoubtedly have heard stories about the tax revolt of 6 A.D., which the Romans had ruthlessly suppressed, and would probably have listened to some of the many apocalyptic preachers who travelled the countryside at that time, among them, most notably, John the Baptist.

Oddly, we know almost as much or more about John the Baptist's background and physical appearance as we do about Jesus'. The two men were opposites in almost every way. John was rough-hewn and entirely lacking in subtlety. He wore a garment woven from camel's hair, had a leather belt about his waist, and apparently lived off the land. He subsisted, we are told, on a diet of locusts and wild honey.

Nor was he given to currying favour with anyone. When a group of Pharisees and Sadducees came to him at the height of his popularity, seeking his baptism, he countered their flattery by asking them who had warned them of the wrath to come. He denounced them as "a generation of vipers," and told them to give proof of their repentance by their actions and not their boastings. "And do not presume to say to yourselves, 'We have Abraham as our father,' " he told them. "God is able from these stones to raise up children to Abraham."

ALTHOUGH WE KNOW A great deal about Jesus' teachings and his ministry, we know virtually nothing about his appearance: whether he was tall or short, fair-skinned or dark-complexioned, heavily or lightly bearded, physically prepossessing or unremarkable. We know nothing of his attire apart from a reference to it during the crucifixion. His outer robe, the text says, was divided by the four soldiers who crucified him. But when they came to his undergarment – which was "without seam, woven from top to bottom" – they said to one another, "Let us not tear it, but cast lots for it to see whose it shall be."

We do know that, following his baptism in the Jordan by John, Jesus began his ministry in Galilee. But for how long a period? The synoptic Gospels seem to indicate that it was for one year, which seems unlikely. John's Gospel says it was for two or more. Early on, he chose twelve men as his apostles and spent much time instructing them, occasionally appearing to be frustrated by their lack of comprehension.

There were many emphases in his preaching but three seem to have been preeminent:

- A conviction that the end of time was near: "Repent," he cried. "The Kingdom of God is at hand."
- Sympathy for the dispossessed, the poor, and the afflicted. "Blessed are the poor in spirit," he said, "for theirs is the Kingdom of Heaven."
- A concern for women and their lot that was uncharacteristic of that era.

In Jesus' time, Jewish women were second-class citizens with few rights and little if any authority. Jesus, however, treated them as equals and women were as likely as men to be the subjects in his parables. He seemed to enjoy the company of women and there were many among his followers. He was especially compassionate toward widows, whose plight in those days was tragic.

He vigorously opposed the Mosaic laws related to divorce. Divorce in the Jewish community was disastrous for the woman, in effect, putting her out on the street with nothing but her personal possessions. A man could – often without just cause and sometimes with no cause at all – "put away" his wife and she subsequently had no claim on him. A woman, on the other hand, was not free to divorce her husband. This inequity may have been the reason why Jesus was so unequivocally negative on the subject of divorce.

He had other unlikely associations: men and women on the fringes of society, outcasts such as prostitutes and adulteresses, lepers, the poor, even the Quislings of that day – Jews who collaborated with the hated Roman government, acting as tax collectors on their behalf. And he assumed an authority that scandalized and enraged the Jewish religious authorities, forgiving sins and performing exorcisms.

JESUS WAS A REVOLUTIONARY in every sense of the word. And he was an iconoclast. He derided the views of the leaders of the society and made no effort to hide his profound disagreements with and occasional scorn for them. "Gentle Jesus, meek and mild" – no description could so misrepresent him. He was a radical in the best sense of that word – out to change people and thus the world. Little wonder the Jewish establishment feared him, came to hate him, set aside their internecine differences and joined forces to plot his death.

His worst offence in their eyes? He spoke of God as "Abba." Abba is an Aramaic word for father and connotes an intimate familial relationship, the relationship of a son to a father perhaps best conveyed in English by the words "Dear Father." It was not the way Jews thought of or spoke of the deity, and was an affront to the orthodox.

Early in his public ministry Jesus drew great crowds. How long he preached in Galilee is unclear, but following the Transfiguration on the Mount, he seemed to realize that the enmities and the opposition he was stirring up would lead to his death and that he must hasten to carry his message to the centre of Jewish culture, Jerusalem. He called the disciples to him – they had been exulting over his burgeoning reputation and extraordinary powers and had even begun to quarrel among themselves about their individual rank in his coming kingdom – and told them his decision.

Then, as the text says, "He set his face toward Jerusalem."

AFTER AN ATTEMPT AT an impressive entry parade into the city, Jesus himself riding a borrowed donkey, his followers shouting hosannas, he taught in the Temple courtyard daily, stimulating both curiosity and hostility. Many were impressed by his words. Some seemed half convinced by his arguments. Others were sceptical. Some challenged him frontally, often, it would seem, at the instigation of the high priest. Invariably Jesus bested his challengers, often answering their questions with questions of his own or with barbed parables. Frequently he used his opponents' own arguments to confound them. And he performed apparently miraculous cures, playing them down, but nonetheless astonishing the onlookers.

His audiences were divided in their reactions, some believing that he might be the Messiah, others insisting that he was a tool of the Devil. Many of the things he said seemed deliberately designed to scandalize the religious authorities. The chief priests and Pharisees were infuriated by his teaching and on more than one occasion dispatched Temple guards to arrest him. But even the guards seemed half convinced and let him be.

As the Passover approached, the hostility of the establishment mounted. The religious leaders met and laid plans to arrest him but hesitated, fearing the reaction of the people. Finally, they managed to bribe one of his apostles, Judas Iscariot, described as the treasurer of the little band, to betray him, paying him thirty pieces of silver. Then, in the early morning hours, outside the city where he had gone to pray in a wooded area known as the Garden of Gethsemane, Jesus was arrested by Roman soldiers and brought before the procurator, Pontius Pilate. As one, his disciples turned craven and fled. Challenged,

and under threat of arrest, Peter, their nominal leader, three times publicly denied so much as knowing Jesus, and sought to authenticate his
denial by cursing.

Pontius Pilate, the Roman procurator of Palestine, apparently
unwilling to come up with the judgement demanded of him by the
priests and Pharisees, passed Jesus on to Herod, the virtual ruler of all
Palestine, arguing that, inasmuch as Jesus was a Galilean, he came
within Herod's jurisdiction. Herod had Jesus brought before him,
amused himself briefly by having sport with him, and then returned
him to Pilate, who, after an attempt of sorts to free him, ordered his
execution by crucifixion, specifying that a sign be posted above Jesus'
head expressly designed to infuriate his accusers. It read: "This is the
King of the Jews."

And there, suspended between heaven and earth, the dream dying,
nailed at the hands and feet to a Roman cross, betrayed by his own
and alone, mocked and derided by the onlookers and passers-by, after
six hours of indescribable and mounting agony, Jesus turned his face
to the heavens and cried out, "My God! My God! . . . Why has *thou*
forsaken me?" and died.

WHAT CAN BE SAID about the New Testament accounts of Jesus'
resurrection? The stories of his cleansing of the Temple, his confrontations with the high priest and the Pharisees, the betrayal by one
of his disciples, his arrest in the Garden of Gethsemane, the farcical
trials by the Romans, and his crucifixion outside the city between two
thieves have about them the sound of authentic history, but the events
that follow do not. As is true of the miraculous events accompanying
his birth, the incidents following his death seem invented and unreal
and do not stand up under scrutiny. The renowned Catholic theologian, Edward Schillebeeckx, explained to an interviewer who had put
the question to him that the resurrection is so alien to human experience, "so apart from human history, that it can only be explained or
understood if one accepts it by an act of faith."

I did exactly that for almost twenty years. I was so irresistibly
drawn to the extraordinary figure of Jesus of Nazareth that when
doubts arose about his divinity I believed my beliefs and doubted my

doubts. It was only when – oh so reluctantly! – I became obedient to the commandment "Thou shalt love the Lord thy God with thy whole *mind*" and began to strip away from the biblical account the accretions of bias and superstition that the injustice and the stark, unutterable horror of the cruel death of this unparalleled human being made its full impact on me.

The Miracles of Jesus

*M*iracles are almost a commonplace in the Old and New Testaments – a total of thirty-five are attributed to Jesus alone. They vary greatly, ranging from what is described as his first miracle, changing water into wine, to healing a variety of physical and emotional afflictions, walking on the water, stilling a storm, feeding five thousand people with a few loaves and fishes, and, the ultimate miracle, raising the dead.

The authors of the Gospels put great emphasis on Jesus' ability to accomplish the miraculous, arguing that these "signs and wonders" are the authentication of his claim to be the Son of God. Jesus himself did not make that emphasis; in fact, he often seemed reluctant, even unwilling, to respond to the entreaties of those seeking his intervention. Nor did he welcome the adulation lavished on him as a result of his reputation as a wonder-worker. Indeed, he often shunned it, apparently believing that it diverted attention from his central message.

When Nicodemus, "a Pharisee, a ruler of the Jews," came to meet with Jesus (under cover of darkness it would seem) he began with a bit of flattery: "Rabbi," he said, "we know that you are a teacher come from God, for no one could do these signs that you do unless God is with him."

Jesus' response was a peremptory changing of the subject and seems of the nature of a rebuke: "Truly, truly, I say to you, unless a man is born anew he cannot see the Kingdom of God."

On another occasion some Pharisees began to hector him, demanding as proof of his mission a sign from heaven, some miracle, some wonder. Jesus sighed deeply and said, "Why does this generation seek a sign? No sign shall be given to it."

On yet another occasion he was accosted by a man described as an official. The man begged him to come and heal his son who was "at the point of death." Jesus said to him – almost wearily, it seems – "Unless you see signs and wonders you will not believe." The man continued to plead: "Sir, come before my child dies." Finally, Jesus responded: "Go; your son will live."

On another occasion, a group brought to him a man who was deaf and had a speech impediment. Jesus took the man aside, spat on his fingers, put them in the man's ears and then touched the man's tongue. Then, raising his eyes to heaven, he said, "Ephphatha!" ("Be open!") Immediately, the text says, "the man's ears were opened, his tongue was loosed, and he spoke plainly." Jesus then said to him firmly, "Tell no one."

The man, of course, told everyone he met.

It seems clear in the Gospels that Jesus wanted to play down his ability to heal and sometimes seemed reluctant to do what was asked of him. Nor is it difficult to understand why. Most of the illnesses that afflict humans were beyond the comprehension of the men and women of that day and, of course, beyond Jesus' comprehension, too. No one at that point in history had even a rudimentary understanding of the causes of physiological or psychological illnesses or of the various other afflictions to which humankind is subject. Most thought of them as punishments from God or the machinations of Satan or other evil spirits.

When, for instance, epilepsy brought on a seizure that caused the victim to collapse and writhe on the ground as though struggling with an internal enemy, when food poisoning produced a paroxysm of vomiting, when a raging fever led to intense shivering and delirium, or when a migraine attack produced visual aberrations and excruciating pain, it seemed reasonable in that prescientific time to interpret such phenomena as the work of an evil spirit. And, when the affliction passed, it was equally reasonable to interpret it as the triumph of a benign spirit over a malign.

Many illnesses, then as now, were psychosomatic and could be "cured" when the sufferer's perception changed. Just as today a placebo prescribed by a physician in whom the patient has faith can effect an apparent cure, so, in an earlier time, faith in the healer could banish adverse symptoms. With each success the healer's reputation would grow and his powers would, as a consequence, become more efficacious.

It would seem evident that this is what happened with Jesus, only in reverse. When he returned to his home town, Nazareth, the reaction there of many of his former neighbours was scepticism.

It is clear in the text that Jesus was seen by the general populace as a wonder-worker. The stories of his exploits went before him – by word of mouth, of course, and thus subject to embellishing – and when he entered a town the state of heightened expectation would often be close to mass hysteria. As a consequence, the apparently miraculous would happen.

Anyone who has watched one of the "healing evangelists" at work in our time will have seen what are touted as "miracles." A state of high excitement is induced. The emotional spigot is turned on by the evangelist's flamboyant style and impassioned entreaties. The presence of the Holy Ghost is announced and the susceptible react with tears, shoutings, agonizing entreaties to God and, not infrequently, with ecstatic trances or physical collapse.

Who among the seekers – desperately needing help for psychological or physiological maladies – can gainsay what they see happening around them? As a result, carried away in a torrent of hyped emotion, and pressured to do so, many claim to be healed.

But do a follow-up the following day and the following week on those who claim to have been – or are announced by the evangelist to have been – healed and you will find almost invariably that, apart from those who were emotionally or psychologically troubled, nothing happened.

The Prayer in Gethsemane

As his final hour approached and the forces opposed to Jesus moved to silence him, it is reported that he gathered the disciples in an upper room in Jerusalem and, after what has been called the Last Supper, spoke to them at length about what lay in store for them and for himself. It is a deeply moving scene and leaves little doubt in the reader's mind that this, in its essence, is an accurate reflection of the authentic Jesus – compassionate, wise, dedicated, and profoundly troubled as he realizes that the end is near. He was, remember, a young man in his early thirties.

It is a painful read – especially the prayer in the seventeenth chapter of John's Gospel – because Jesus seems to be aware that, within hours, he will be dead and his followers scattered and persecuted, even driven, as Peter and Judas were, to betray him.

It is evident, however, that Jesus' prayer in the Garden of Gethsemane is an imagined reconstruction of the event by the authors. Although the Gospels of Matthew, Mark, and Luke present what purport to be eyewitness accounts of what Jesus said and did in the garden, the text makes it obvious that their accounts differ and cannot be factual.

All three state that, having gone with the disciples to the garden, Jesus went off by himself. "Sit here," he told them, "while I go and pray yonder." He then "parted from them a stone's throw," and, therefore, beyond earshot. Yet, despite the apparent impossibility of his having been overheard – much less his words inscribed – Matthew's

Gospel quotes verbatim the words of his prayer: "My father, if it be possible, let this cup pass from me. . . . Nevertheless, not as I will but as thou wilt."

Moreover, although it was dark and they were in a treed area and Jesus was a stone's-throw distance away, the apostles report seeing "his sweat, like great drops of blood, falling on the ground."

That they could not have overheard his prayer is made further evident by the statement that "when [Jesus] rose up from his prayer, he came unto the disciples and found them asleep." Three times, the records state, he withdrew to pray, and three times he returned to find the disciples asleep. The third time he said to them, "Sleep on. Take your rest."

It would seem that Jesus did not *want* his prayer overheard. If he had, would he have distanced himself from the apostles after specifically instructing them to stand watch where they were?

THERE ARE FURTHER problems with the story. Christian teaching asserts that Jesus is the Son of God, the Second Person of the Holy Trinity, Very God of Very God, and that the reason for his coming to the world was to purchase the redemption of humankind by the sacrifice of his life.

But the reported prayer in Gethsemane is at odds with this.

In his prayer Jesus pleads with the Father to abort the divine plan, saying again and again, "If it be possible, remove this cup from me." This would be a reasonable reaction in a human being, but Jesus is presented as much more than that; he is the manifestation in human flesh of the Godhead. Moreover, the stated reason for his coming to earth as a human being was that he might die for the sins of humankind. Why then would he now want to abandon his reason for being?

But there is a larger, theological reason for questioning the story. Why would an all-wise, loving, and compassionate Father require the agonizing death of his Son as the means to achieve the forgiveness of the sins of mortal men? It was done, theologians tell us, to satisfy divine law. But is not God the Father the originator of the law? The concept reduces Jesus' death to no more than the ultimate extension of the primitive "an eye for an eye, a tooth for a tooth, a life for a life" principle. In early history justice was seen to be done only if a penalty equal to the infraction was exacted. Having murdered, the murderer is himself slain.

A life for a life, a death for a death. Scales balanced.

The Christian plan of salvation is predicated on this primitive notion of justice. "The wages of sin is death," says the apostle Paul, therefore the sinner must die. But, the argument goes, Jesus the man – who was himself without sin – died in our stead, and if we "accept him as Saviour and Lord" we pass from condemnation to eternal life for he has paid our debt.

A life for a life, a death for a death. Scales balanced.

But the equation won't bear examination. If Jesus was truly a man (and the incarnation was no more than a charade if he wasn't) then his substitutionary sacrifice, his individual death, would be efficacious for only one individual – certainly not *for all humankind!*

Moreover, if one accepts it as fact that Jesus actually did take to himself our sins, he died a sinner and would, as a consequence, himself be damned: "The wages of sin is death."

But the intrinsic problems in the story go beyond this: If "the wages of sin is death," and if "there is no other name under heaven given among men whereby you must be saved," then the preponderance of the men and women who have lived and died since the dawn of time are in hell. Throughout history only a small portion of the world's population has been Christian or has so much as heard the Christian message. Of the approximately 5.6 billion people now alive only a small portion call themselves Christian, which means that billions now living are on their way to hell – not to mention the billions throughout history who lived and died without having so much as *heard* of Jesus!

The Christian concept of the universal need for divine forgiveness (and, failing that, the eternal punishment of the sinner) is not only illogical, it is nonsensical. And if Jesus' mission on earth was to reconcile humankind to God, any objective judgement would have to conclude that it was a failure.

Indeed, God's plan of salvation, as it is called, has been a series of disasters from Day One. In the beginning the deity entrusted his truth solely to a small Middle Eastern nomadic people, the Jews. But, instead of sharing the words of life, they jealously husbanded them. It was only after the passage of thousands of years that gentiles began to be accepted. Under the New Testament part of the plan, Jesus commanded his followers to "go into all the world and preach the Gospel to every creature," but centuries passed before the influence of Christianity on the world was at all significant. Even today, Christianity is only one of the many major religions of the world.

The Resurrection

As we have seen, the stories of Jesus' birth are demonstrably legends. And the same is true of the events that followed his death. The accounts in the Gospels of the last week of his life resonate with the ring of authenticity, but even the most sympathetic reading of the events following his death will leave an unbiased reader convinced that they are fables, addenda put forward by his followers hoping to keep the dream alive.

Let us examine the record.

In summary, the New Testament states that Jesus of Nazareth, having been put on trial by the Roman government and found guilty, having been publicly flogged and then crucified by Roman soldiers, was pronounced dead and his body taken down from the cross and consigned for burial to a wealthy follower, one Joseph of Arimathea.

Watched by Mary Magdalene and Mary the mother of James and Joses, Joseph of Arimathea wrapped the body in a fine linen shroud, embalmed it with one hundred pounds of myrrh and aloes, placed it in the tomb he had purchased earlier for his own use, and had a great stone rolled in front of the entrance.

The record states that the chief priests and the Pharisees were not satisfied with this, however. They went to Pilate and insisted that the tomb be sealed. If not, they warned, his disciples would spirit away the body and claim that he has risen from the dead. Pilate responded: "You have a guard of soldiers. Take care of it yourselves." So they sealed the tomb.

But, according to the four Gospels, this was not the end of the story. They assert that, sometime over the weekend, Jesus came back to life and was in a nearby garden when Mary Magdalene came at dawn the following morning to lay flowers at the grave. Moreover, they record that the resurrected Jesus made an appearance to men on the outskirts of the town of Emmaus and on numerous other occasions in Jerusalem, Galilee, and elsewhere.

But let us keep the story in perspective. If the accounts in the Gospels are true, Jesus' return to life would have been a miracle unparalleled in history and word of it would have spread throughout Palestine within hours. *A dead man, certifiably alive!* Hundreds of people from the city would have thronged to the tomb to see for themselves and word of the miracle would have spread like wildfire throughout Palestine.

There is, however, not a mention of it in any of the secular histories of the time. Not a word. Moreover, a careful examination of the Gospel accounts of his resurrection leads inescapably to the conclusion that they lack authenticity, are mutually contradictory, were written long after Jesus' death and are no more than legends.

NOTE SOME OF THE discrepancies and contradictions in the four Gospels:

Early Sunday morning, on the third day after the crucifixion, a number of women followers went to the sepulchre where Jesus had been buried, intending, as was common practice, to anoint the body with fragrant spices, a means used to cover the odour of a body's decomposition. John's account says it was still dark, Luke's says it was early dawn, Mark's says the sun had risen.

Matthew says that Mary Magdalene went to the tomb accompanied by "the other Mary." Mark says there were not two but three women: Mary Magdalene, Mary the mother of James, and a woman named Salome. Luke adds still others: Joanna and "the other women with them." John says that Mary Magdalene went to the tomb not once but twice, and that she went alone.

To return to Matthew's account: it states that Sunday morning, just before dawn, Mary Magdalene and the other Mary went to the tomb. It states further that there was a major earthquake and that an angel descended from heaven, broke the seal, rolled away the stone that blocked the entrance to the tomb and sat upon it. The angel's appearance, we are told, "was like lightning, his raiment was white as snow and, for fear of him, the guards trembled and became like dead men."

The angel tells the women not be afraid, takes Mary Magdalene and the other Mary into the empty tomb, shows them the place where Jesus had lain and tells them to go quickly and tell the disciples that Jesus has risen, gone to Galilee, and will meet them there. Frightened, but ecstatic, the women run to carry the good news to the disciples.

But Mark's, Luke's, and John's Gospels make no reference to an earthquake, nor is there any mention of it in the secular histories of the time.

Mark's account states that on the Sunday, at sunrise, Mary Magdalene, with the other Mary and a third woman, Salome, find the stone rolled away from the entrance to the tomb and a young man dressed in a white robe seated, not on the stone but inside the tomb. The young man – presumably an angel – tells the women that Jesus has risen and gone to Galilee and that they should inform the disciples that he will meet them there.

Frightened, the three women flee the tomb. And even though they have been specifically instructed by an angel to tell "the disciples and Peter," they tell no one. Mark's account states that Mary Magdalene later told the apostles but that none of them believed her.

Luke's Gospel says that Mary Magdalene, Joanna, Mary the mother of James, and "some other women" go to the tomb on the Sunday morning and find it empty. This time two angels materialize before them "in dazzling apparel." Terrified, the women fall to their knees, faces to the ground. The angels ask why they have come seeking the living in a place of death and inform them that Jesus has risen. The women go immediately to Jerusalem, where the apostles and others are hiding, and tell them what has happened, but their report is dismissed as idle rumour. Nonetheless, Peter, apparently alone, runs to the tomb, sees the linen binding-cloths but no body and no angels and, puzzled, returns to his home.

John's Gospel says that Mary Magdalene went alone to the tomb, found the stone rolled away, and ran to tell Peter and John that someone has removed Jesus' body. Peter, this time accompanied by John, runs to the tomb and sees the binding-cloths but no body, whereupon, he and John proceed to their homes.

Mary Magdalene bends over to look into the tomb and sees two angels, one at the head and one at the foot of the sarcophagus. When the angels ask why she is weeping, she replies, "Because they have taken away my Lord's body and I don't know where it is."

As she is speaking to the angels within the tomb, she turns around and sees Jesus but doesn't recognize him. He says, "Woman, why are you weeping? Whom are you looking for?" Taking him to be the gardener, she says, "Sir, if you have carried him away, tell me where you have laid him and I will take him away." Jesus then says one word, "Mary!" She responds, "Teacher!" "Don't cling to me," Jesus says. "I have not yet ascended to the Father. But go to my brothers and say to them, I am ascending to my Father and your Father, to my God and your God." Mary Magdalene then goes to where the disciples are hiding and tells them that she has seen and talked with the Lord.

AS IS EVIDENT, THE four descriptions of events after the resurrection differ so markedly at so many points that, with all the good will in the world, they cannot be reconciled. Moreover, they are completely at odds with the apostle Paul's account in I Corinthians. He states that the resurrected Jesus appeared first, not to Mary Magdalene, but to Peter and then to the Twelve. He then, Paul adds, appeared to more than five hundred of the brethren at one time, then to James, then to all the apostles ". . . and last of all, he appeared also to me."

But according to the Gospels, this is not at all what happened. Paul makes no mention of *any* woman, but the Gospels say that *only women* were first at the burial site. And John specifically states that it was not Peter but Mary Magdalene who first saw the resurrected Jesus – at which time the disciples were hiding out in Jerusalem.

There are even more contradictions.

Eight days after the crucifixion the disciples are said to have been in hiding in a room in Jerusalem. Suddenly Jesus materialized in their midst. The disciples were certain they were seeing a ghost but Jesus showed them the wound in his side and the scars on his hands and feet and said, "You can be sure it is I – ghosts aren't flesh and blood which, as you can see, I am." He then demonstrated that he was not an apparition by inviting them to touch him and by eating a piece of broiled fish in their presence.

WE COME AT THIS point to what is an addition to the text of John's Gospel, obviously appended later by someone unnamed. The locale moves from Jerusalem to the Sea of Tiberias in Galilee. Peter, Thomas, Nathanael, the brothers James and John, and two other disciples are sitting talking. Peter gets to his feet. "I'm going fishing," he says. "Wait," they say, "we'll all go."

They fish all night but catch nothing. As day breaks, Jesus is seen standing on the beach but is not recognized. He calls out: "Children, have you any fish?" They answered him, "No." He said to them, "Cast the net on the right side of the boat and you will find some." There follows a near duplication of the earlier story about the miraculous draught of fishes. The disciples bring the catch ashore but "none of them dared to ask him, 'Who are you?' They knew it was the Lord."

But why not? He had sent a message through Mary, the mother of James and Salome, to meet them in Galilee. Moreover, according to Luke, they had just come from being with him in Jerusalem. They have met with him, talked to him, touched him, seen his wounds, watched him eat, and been reassured by him, so why would they now ask, "Who are you?"

There is a further implausibility in the resurrection account. Matthew's Gospel reports that, at the moment of Jesus' death there was a major earthquake. The veil of the Temple was torn from top to bottom and there was a mass resurrection of the dead – men and women came out of their graves, went into Jerusalem, "and were seen by many."

But this is not credible. If such a miraculous event actually did take place, how could Matthew dismiss it with a sentence? Why, moreover, are none of these resurrected men and women named? They were members of the Christian community and would have been known to the others. And why is such an unheard-of phenomenon not so much as mentioned in any of the other Gospels or in any of the secular histories of that time? You could not keep such an event secret for an hour! Here, in the capital city of Jerusalem, in the flesh, alive and ecstatic with excitement, is a group of resurrected men and women, fresh from the grave with the answers to life's ultimate questions, and no one lists any of their names or seems to have asked them what happens after death, or, if they did, thought the information of sufficient importance to pass it on.

Let the reader imagine the scene: The astonished spectators, the gathering crowd, the family members and friends, weeping and delirious with excitement. Surely someone would have plied them with questions: "What happened as you died?" "Did you see God?" "What is Heaven like?" "Were you reunited with your parents and other members of your family?" Surely the answers to these and other questions like them would have flashed across Palestine within hours and been recorded *somewhere*. But there is not one word of it in history.

The entire resurrection story is not credible.

The Ascension

*T*he stories in the Gospels describing Jesus' ascension into Heaven differ from each other so fundamentally that an unbiased reader will recognize them for what they are: an attempt by early Christians to add a happy ending to the tragic story of Jesus' death.

The reader should bear in mind what the Gospels are asserting. They are claiming that a man, executed, certified dead, buried in a sealed tomb and guarded by Roman soldiers, got out of the tomb on the morning of the third day and, following a series of meetings with his disciples over forty days, went with them to a nearby mountainside, levitated into the sky, disappeared in a cloud, and took a seat on a throne at the right hand of God the Father.

The resurrection, if factual, would be an event unique in the history of the world. If Jesus had risen from the grave and, before the eyes of his followers, ascended to Heaven, would not those who witnessed it remember in meticulous detail every word spoken and everything that transpired? But check the record.

Matthew's Gospel spends more time claiming that the chief priests bribed the graveyard guards to say that Jesus' followers had stolen the body than it does describing all of Jesus' post-resurrection appearances, referring only indirectly to the ascension.

Mark's Gospel does not mention the ascension. Luke's Gospel, after a disclaimer stating that he was not an eyewitness but is simply passing on what he has been able to learn through his research, then presumes to quote verbatim not only what Jesus said but entire conversations, including what Jesus' respondents said. He concludes by stating that the resurrected Jesus, after meeting with the apostles in Jerusalem "led them out as far as Bethany and, lifting up his hands, he blessed them and parted from them."

John's Gospel does not so much as mention the ascension.

A report in the Acts of the Apostles (commonly attributed to Luke) goes further than the others but is in conflict with Luke's Gospel at a number of points. It states that, after the resurrection, Jesus met with his disciples many times over a period of forty days, instructing them to stay in Jerusalem until they have been empowered by the Holy Ghost for ministry. He then led them outside Jerusalem to the Mount of Olives and, "as they were watching, a cloud took him out of their sight." Two men in white robes materialize and inform them that "this Jesus who has been taken up from you into heaven, will come in the same way as you saw him go into heaven."

The major inconsistencies and contradictions in the stories of Jesus' birth and resurrection (as distinct from his ministry) make it obvious that they are the imaginings of Christians whose purposes were to authenticate the claims being made by the early church.

The Christian Church

The Christian Church

The Christian church is very much like:

The little girl who had a little curl
Right in the middle of her forehead.
And when she was good she was very very good,
But when she was bad she was horrid.

The record of the Christian church is a checkered one. Over twenty centuries it has done immeasurable good. It has ministered to the sick, the dying, and the bereaved, built schools and hospitals, cared for the dispossessed, fed the hungry, brought enlightenment to illiterate and impoverished peoples, run endless errands of mercy, and otherwise improved the lives of millions.

In its ranks, men and women like Florence Nightingale, Mother Theresa, David Livingstone, William and Catherine Booth, and innumerable others have demonstrated love in action. They represent the church at its best.

But the church has seldom been at its best. Too often it has been a negative influence. Too often it has stood in the way of progress. Too often it has made women second-class humans, subsidiary to and subservient to men. Over most of the two thousand years since Jesus of Nazareth lived and died, it has denied women equality, barred them from ordination and the priesthood, and treated them as inferior. This bias has been rectified belatedly by the Protestant churches, but the largest Christian communion of them all, the Roman church, remains mired in its antiquated male-chauvinist attitude about admission to the priesthood.

THE TERM "THE CHRISTIAN church" is a misnomer. The Christian church as an entity does not exist. There is a plethora of denominations, organizations, fellowships, movements, congregations, groups, assemblies, bands, and cells – even an "army," the Salvation Army. Many of them are poles apart in theology and practice. The breadth and depth of their lack of oneness can be glimpsed when one compares, say, the thirty thousand Roman Catholics gathered on an Easter Sunday morning for a High Mass outside St. Peter's in Rome with the half-dozen handclapping, hallelujah-shouting Full Gospel adherents in a tiny frame church in the American South. The two groups are antithetical in every way but one: they each worship the God of the Bible.

There are approximately 1.6 billion Christian men and women related to a bewildering variety of Christian communions around the world. They include:

- A sparse group of elderly men and women attending a Lenten service in an Anglican cathedral in London and a jam-packed crowd of boisterous hyper-enthusiasts in a Full Gospel church close to the Toronto airport.
- A Salvation Army officer ringing his hand-bell as he solicits contributions from passers-by in a Liverpool street and a group of Seventh Day Adventists gathering for a service in Los Angeles on a Saturday, their Sabbath.
- A shivering group of bundled-up Eastern Orthodox worshippers fingering their prayer beads in an ornate but freezing-cold temple in Moscow and a scattering of solemn worshippers, heads bowed, in an unornamented Quaker meeting house in Philadelphia.
- A solemn group of Amish Mennonites in Zurich joined in silent prayer and a Full Gospel preacher enthusiastically immersing new converts in a baptismal tank in Seoul, South Korea.

- A decorous and well-dressed group of worshippers in an Episcopal cathedral in Chicago and a jam-packed Jehovah's Witness rally in a rented sports arena in London.
- A band of Southern Baptist teenagers passing out tracts door-to-door in Texas and a small group of Holy Ghost Christians in Kentucky handling venomous snakes as proof of their faith.
- The Mormon Tabernacle Choir, their voices raised in song in Salt Lake City, and a few miles out of town a group of dissident Mormons, expelled by the mother church because they will not abandon polygamy, which, at one time, the church approved.
- In Boston, a solemn and dignified Unitarian congregation and, not far away, a Pentecostal church where the members speak in tongues, run up and down the aisles, emit strange sounds in a spiritual ecstasy, or are "slain of the Lord."

And anywhere in the Western world you can turn on a television set and shake your head in wonder at the fulminating salesmanship of a sweaty television evangelist as he rails against sin in one breath and in the next pleads with even greater fervour for "love offerings" from members he has never seen.

And despite the fact that Jesus enjoined his followers to love one another, most don't, each believing that only they have seen the true light of the Gospel and that all the others are in error.

ACROSS THE CENTURIES and on every continent, Christians – the followers of the Prince of Peace – have been the cause of and involved in strife. The clergy have sanctified arms and armies and asked the blessing of God on soldiers as they went forth to kill and destroy other human beings, many of them Christians, in the name of the loving God. In the name of the loving God Christians have persecuted other Christians, imprisoned some, publicly condemned others, and burned at the stake those who differed with or opposed them, or who merely interpreted the scriptures differently.

And throughout history Christians have killed one another in bloody wars.

The physical violence has diminished with the centuries but the divisions continue – and proliferate. Once there was a single Christian group, Jesus of Nazareth's tiny band of twelve apostles; now there are thousands. It has been estimated that there are some twenty-two thousand separate and distinct Christian groups around the world.

Not to suggest that all Christians contend with other Christians: a number of the oldest and largest churches have formally joined with others of like mind to establish organizations such as the World Council of Churches, the Canadian Council of Churches and the National Council of Christian Churches in the U.S.A. But, even while these belated efforts to broaden Christian fellowship are being made, the membership and the influence of the Christian church continues to decline at an accelerating rate.

There was a time – and not long ago – when the clergy counselled kings and parliaments. No longer. In the West and in most of Europe the church no longer speaks with an effective voice. Lip-service is paid by most of the secular power structures and church functionaries are invited to participate on great state occasions, but they are there on sufferance and are no longer the power behind the throne.

The glory has departed.

As a consequence, the impress of the church on the life of the community is swiftly diminishing. One of the reasons for this declining influence is the failure of the church to speak relevantly to its adherents or to help them deal effectively with their everyday problems. Many who once turned to the local clergyman for counsel now visit a marriage counsellor, psychologist, or psychiatrist. Increasingly, public worship is seen by members of the church as being of less importance than family, friends, service clubs, and leisure. The failing away from England's official faith, Anglicanism, has reached such crisis proportions that, although the church has the nominal support of some 60 per cent of the country's population, only 4 per cent of Britons regularly attend Sunday services.

Even in Ireland, that "jewel in the papacy's crown," there is clear evidence of a major decline. Father Gabriel Daly, a lecturer in theology at Dublin's Trinity College, states it succinctly: "We are rapidly turning into a more secular society." Opinion polls reveal that a majority of the Roman Catholic laity in Ireland favours ending the restrictions on contraception, divorce, and homosexual relations between consenting adults. The government – once dominated by the church – has held two referendums on divorce; the second, in 1995, narrowly found in favour of legalization.

IN WHAT APPEARS TO BE an accelerating and irreversible trend, Canadian churches are declining in both membership and church attendance. A recent Angus Reid–*Maclean's* magazine poll revealed that, while some 86 per cent of Canadians say they believe in God, only 24 per cent trouble to attend church weekly: or, by denomination, only 16 per cent of Anglicans, 20 per cent of United Church members, and 30 per cent of Catholics. Moreover, because these figures are responses to a query from a stranger about the individual's religious commitment, it is likely that these numbers are inflated. Even among fundamentalists, the proportion of the members attending church on Sundays is down 50 per cent in recent decades.

A 1992 Gallup poll noted that only one in three Canadians had attended a church, synagogue, or place of worship the previous week. Earlier polls indicate that this is a new low in what appears to be a continuing decline. In 1957 the figure stood at fully 60 per cent – a drop of almost 50 per cent in thirty-five years.

Tom Harpur, the distinguished author and *Toronto Star* columnist on religious matters, writes: "Experienced observers of the religious life of this country know that if you were to project on even the roughest kind of graphs the curve of where church membership is headed – and has been steadily since the late 50s – you would see that *total extinction* [his emphasis] is a real possibility before 2050. It doesn't matter if 78 per cent (a *Maclean's* poll) or 100 per cent tell the census taker-pollster that they are United, Anglican, Roman Catholic or whatever, if one day soon, only an aging few find his or her church sufficiently relevant to merit attendance and support."

Congregations in the established churches are aging. Sunday-morning worshippers are older on average than the population as a whole and comprise more women than men. Only 24 per cent of the respondents are between the ages of eighteen and twenty-nine while twice that number are sixty-five or older. The 1992 Gallup poll revealed also that only three of every ten Canadians trouble to pray daily and only one in five reads the Bible regularly. Indeed, 40 per cent of Canadians categorize themselves variously as non-Christian, agnostic, atheist, or indifferent.

Prior to this poll, the United Church of Canada announced in its official publication, *The Observer*, that it had culled almost twenty-three thousand from its membership rolls in 1991. A similar decline in active commitment is evident in the traditional churches in the United States. And there, too, the membership is aging.

ONE OF THE POSITIVE changes in Protestant churches is the hard-won concession that admits women to leadership roles. From their beginnings, Jew and Christians – in company with most other religionists, and, indeed, the Holy Bible – treated women as a lesser breed. The Roman Catholic church, despite its token elevation of the Virgin Mary to veneration, has repeatedly and adamantly refused to allow women to fill any of the sacramental offices of the church. The Church of England – as recently as November 1992 and only after centuries of inflexible refusal – has finally agreed to the ordination of women priests, a decision that led immediately to the threat of a mass resignation by a large number of the clergy. Seven bishops and more than seven hundred clerics have indicated that they plan to convert to Roman Catholicism if the church does not reverse its position. The Anglican church in Canada moved to ordain women in 1976.

IN THE PAST HALF-CENTURY, in Europe and in much of North America, the influence of the churches on the daily life of society has diminished dramatically. Only a few decades ago – as the Christian majority imposed its will – the "closed Sunday" was the norm. Sunday was the "Lord's Day" and a "day of rest." Church pews were crowded. All but essential businesses were closed by law. Theatres and places of amusement were dark.

Today, there are broad expanses of empty pews on Sunday mornings and a majority of churches have dropped evening worship entirely. The "wide open" Sunday flourishes. The Sunday-morning travesties of many of the television evangelists have diminished –

much of that decline a result of a series of bizarre sexual and monetary scandals.

Beyond question, the influence of the church on society is waning. Politicians who used to dance to the tune piped by the clergy and who invariably concluded their public perorations with a *de rigueur* reference to the deity, no longer trouble to.

IT SHOULD BE UNDERSTOOD that those leaving the church are not necessarily saying farewell to God. When, in Western Europe, men and women quit the church, many abandon their traditional religious beliefs as well, but North Americans do not invariably turn to agnosticism or atheism. This is especially true of the young. Wade Ciak Roof, a sociologist at the University of California, did a broad survey of American baby-boomers who have abandoned the traditional churches, and in his book *A Generation of Seekers*, he reports that some 25 per cent of those who quit the church do not dismiss their religious beliefs but continue in their search for some kind of spiritual values. Many continue to believe in God but he is not the austere God of the Old Testament or the ritualized God of the traditional churches. Some are drawn to the highly informal services of the evangelistic churches. Others are investigating Eastern religions, New Age teaching, reincarnation theory, astrology, and other unconventional faiths.

It should be noted that even as the North American and European churches are diminishing in numbers and influence, fundamentalists are making inroads in what was not long ago thought of as the non-Christian world. Some eighty-one thousand Protestant Christian missionaries of all denominations are at work in what is called "the foreign field," many with some success. In the past, Christian foreign missions were dominated by the old-line churches, but in recent years, others – especially the evangelicals and Pentecostals – appear to be making sizable incursions.

The growth of evangelicalism has been largest in Asia, Latin America, South Korea, Brazil, and central East Africa. Indeed, South Korea boasts the world's largest Christian church: half a million members belong to the Full Gospel church in Seoul. American evangelist

Billy Graham's Crusade registered the largest total attendance in the organization's history in Seoul.

THERE ARE, AS WAS NOTED earlier, approximately twenty-two thousand separate and distinct Christian groups around the world. The largest among them and the largest of all the world's organized religions is the Roman Catholic church, with 900 million members. The next largest, the Eastern Orthodox church (158 million), is the result of the split of the Roman church in the fifth century.

Among Western churches the various Baptists, with their 31 million members, are the largest, the Church of England ranks second with 20 million – with some 2.7 million more if one includes the American Episcopalians. The Methodists come next with 13.5 million, followed by the Lutherans with 8 million.

None of the others approaches these numbers. There are 3.5 million Pentecostals, 3.2 million Presbyterians, 2.8 million Mormons, 1.7 million members of the United Church of Christ, and 1.6 million who belong to the Church of Christ. There are some 700,000 Jehovah's Witnesses and 113,000 members in the Religious Society of Friends (Quakers).

Judaism has some 18 million followers.

It should be borne in mind when assessing these numbers that in some cases they bear little resemblance to actuality. The number of members claimed by every religious body is almost invariably exaggerated, particularly if one includes only those who are active in the church or who regularly attend services.

It is commonly believed that Christians outnumber members of the other religions of the world. There are in fact many more followers of other faiths.

Non-Christian religionists number approximately 2 billion worldwide, with Islam the largest group (840 million), Hinduism the second-largest (648 million), followed by Buddhism (307 million). Shinto, the long-established religion of Japan, emphasizes a belief in numerous spiritual beings and gods known as *kami* and has 3.5 million followers. It is not possible to specify the number of adherents to Taoism, a Chinese religion, for it is not published. Taoism is both a religion and a philosophy and, despite being actively discouraged by the government of the People's Republic of China, it continues to flourish. It also has many followers in Taiwan.

ONE OF THE PARADOXICAL aspects of the Christian church (with its emphasis on love) is that, throughout history, Christians have contended vigorously with each other in internecine quarrels over points of doctrine or practice. Jesus' disciples disputed with one another over who would be first in the Kingdom of Heaven and had to be rebuked. The apostle Paul – differing from Peter on the best approach to gentiles – wrote in Galatians: "When Peter came to Antioch I opposed him to his face, because he stood condemned . . ."

Raised in a particular denomination or group, many judge others' behaviour by their acceptance or rejection of certain "proof texts" or by their form of worship and often brand as heretical or apostate those who differ from them.

Divisions have arisen over such matters as whether the Bible is the inerrant and infallible Word of God, whether a convert has been properly baptized if he has been sprinkled or poured rather than immersed, whether someone has had a genuine born-again experience, whether one must be sanctified after having been converted, whether a convert must speak in other tongues as validation that he or she has been baptized with the Holy Ghost, whether Saturday or Sunday is the proper day for worship, whether women should be ordained, hear confessions, or officiate, whether a man may have more than one wife, whether there should be an ordained clergy.

The list is long.

THE ONLY PROTESTANT groups that have held their own and, in a few cases, increased their numbers in the twentieth century are the fundamentalist churches. Fundamentalists – Bible-believing Christians as they call themselves (with its implied rebuke) – have been exceptions to the general decline of the church. As their description of themselves indicates, they cling to what they call "the old-time religion," the underlying principle of which is the unequivocal assertion that the Bible is the literal Word of God. They condemn as modernists or apostate Christians who don't agree. They reject any advance in science or learning that contradicts the Genesis account of the creation of the world, the disobedience of Adam and Eve in the Garden of Eden, and God's curse on the world and humankind. They believe that the only deliverance from this curse and eventual banishment to an eternal hell is to be "born again."

Most fundamentalist preaching has a high emotional content. The delivery is passionate. It has been said of a prominent fundamentalist orator: "What he lacks in lightning he makes up for in thunder." The objective is to induce feelings of guilt and win converts. The unconverted – commonly categorized as "sinners" – are often intimidated by fear of the judgement of God and the certainty of eternal punishment in a fire-and-brimstone hell unless they "accept Jesus Christ as their personal Saviour," following which, the way of escape is offered: accept God's gift of eternal life through Jesus Christ and be saved.

It is not a faith for the scholar or the contemplative.

Fundamentalist preaching may and sometimes does induce a dramatically changed life, but its converts tend to be judgemental and elitist. And fundamentalism deadens the mind. Who can measure the psychological warping that can stem from constant exposure to a black/white, right/wrong, sinner/saved outlook on life?

The negative emphasis of fundamentalist preaching sometimes does serious harm. Complex choices are portrayed as black or white. Adam's sin is often interpreted as being sexual – which, of course, it was not. Even masturbation is condemned as a sin against Almighty God.

As well, there are "the sins of omission" – the failure to do something "good" – such as faithfully saying one's prayers or giving one's testimony at every opportunity. Many so-called sins are no more than the normal – and inevitable – sexual experiments of the young on reaching puberty. Other sins are no more than failures of restraint or moments of weakness. But the unremitting and frequently thunderous denunciations of sin from the pulpit can in some circumstances produce deep feelings of guilt and inflict serious emotional damage.

There are, it must be added, those vacuous preachers at the opposite pole in the old-line churches whose exhortations to righteousness are so vague and vapid and so far removed from Jesus' teaching as to be unrecognizable as the Christian Good News. These religio-philosophical musings are often more a soporific than a call to commitment. They do, however, have one virtue: they are usually brief. Nonetheless, a near-miracle has happened: a man has talked about God for twenty minutes without either inspiring or infuriating anyone.

Jesus himself couldn't do that.

The Plan of Salvation

What is one required to believe in order to become a member of the Christian church? With some denominational variations it is summed up as follows:

I believe in God the Father, the Creator of Heaven and Earth, and in Jesus Christ his Son, born of the Virgin Mary, who suffered under Pontius Pilate, was crucified, dead and buried. He arose on the third day and ascended into Heaven where he sits at the right hand of God the Father, from whence he shall come to judge the quick and the dead. I believe in the Holy Ghost, the Holy Catholic (universal) Church, and in life everlasting.

This declaration of faith is predicated on three assumptions:

- That sin is a transgression of the law of God.
- That all have sinned and come short of the glory of God.
- That the wages of sin is death but the gift of God is eternal life.

Adam's disobedience in Eden was followed by God's curse on Adam and his seed. Christian religious leaders saw it as requisite to establish a plan of salvation that would satisfy both Mosaic law and the teachings of Jesus of Nazareth, make the sinner righteous in the eyes of God and worthy of God's gift of eternal life. It was a giant step beyond the provisions of the Mosaic law – which had been created at a time in history when violence was a way of life and life was "nasty, brutish, and short." A wise leader, Moses – realizing that violence begot violence and that violence unrestrained led to anarchy and possibly to extinction – established a set of laws, based on ten fundamental Commandments, and carved them in stone – attributing them to Yahweh himself.

Wickedness in general and violence in particular were seen by Moses not simply as disobedience of the laws of men but as a flouting of the laws of God – transgressions to be absolved only by the shedding of the blood of sacrificial animals by a priest, by specific penalties in this world, and, for the unrepentant, by eternal death in the world to come. In that relatively primitive time it was an effective way to establish an orderly society.

Centuries later, this violent, retributive system of justice informed an emerging Christian theology. Jesus of Nazareth, the Christian church asserted, outmoded the Mosaic system and replaced it with the concept that humankind needed no longer to approach God through an intermediary and by the sacrifice of a living creature, but had direct access to the Father through his Son, the Second Person of the Holy Trinity. By offering himself as the sacrifice to end all sacrifices, the sinless Jesus satisfied the justice of God, and when the individual confessed his sins and accepted Jesus Christ as his Saviour, he was born again as a child of God, inherited the Son's eternal life, and thus escaped the penalty for sin, eternal death.

Inspired by the substitutionary death of Jesus, this new approach to the problem of sin and eternal death gave birth to a new religion, Christianity, the influence of which, across two thousand years, has been immeasurable.

But that day is passing. God is no longer conceived of by most as an omniscient and omnipresent deity; he is a remote figure, a revered but amorphous concept. His words are little remembered and his will is seldom considered. How often on a given day does the average Christian pause before taking a specific action to consider whether God will approve it? The fact is that, in contemporary life – apart from an increasingly infrequent hour in church on Sunday mornings – the Christian church is dying.

Our Outdated Heritage

*T*he church calls the Bible the Word of God but, apart from the fundamentalists, not many of the clergy or many laymen take the term literally. The Bible is a fascinating compilation of Jewish and early Christian history and, because of the sweep of the story and the majesty of the language, a unique treasure. We swear by it in court, read portions of it at christenings, weddings, and funerals, and quote from it during the high holidays of Christmas and Easter. But how many thoughtful men and women in our time believe that the Bible is the very Word of God and take particular pains to obey its teachings in their daily lives?

In simple truth it has become outdated.

Does the seventh Commandment deter the adulterer? Does the fifth give pause to the stock manipulator? Does the eighth induce the truth when a lie is convenient? How many these days remember the Sabbath day, to keep it holy? Do we abjure coveting because the Bible forbids it – coveting, for example, one's neighbour's wife or his house or his new car or his bank account? Do we take care not to put any other God before the God of the Bible?

Mammon, for instance? Or Aphrodite?

THE REALITY IS THAT some of Jesus' teachings are a counsel of perfection. Taken literally and followed in our contemporary world they would be disastrous.

Consider: Jesus told his disciples to love their enemies, and then added: "Do not resist someone who is evil. If someone strikes you on the right cheek, turn to him the other also." Try that in downtown Los Angeles and the muggers may not be finished with you until you are on your way to the nearest hospital.

Jesus said: "If someone would take your coat, let him have your cloak also." Do that in the slum neighbourhoods of London and you will be stripped to your underwear in minutes.

"Give to him who begs from you, and do not refuse him who would borrow from you." Do this in any of the great cities of the world and every beggar and deadbeat in town will be at your door within the hour. Jesus went on to say, if someone steals your property don't demand its return. In a contemporary context, when your wallet is stolen, should you give the thief your car keys? And if he then demands the keys to your house?

In today's world, such behaviour would put you on the fast track to penury.

Jesus' teaching, "Love your enemy," is a counsel of perfection. Surely he did not intend to convey the idea that you should feel affection for someone out to do you harm. In today's world the word "love" has a different connotation. Love describes the profound attachment of a mother for her child or a man for his wife or that unique identification with each other that members of a family feel. It is impossible to summon this emotion for the person whose hatred or rapacity or meanness has earned your enmity.

The magnanimity of spirit that Jesus advocated might make it possible to understand, even empathize with, a man whose actions are evil, but if he moves from one assault to the next it would not only be impossible to love him, it would be wrong. Society should be protected from his rapacity. Not to lock him up would be needlessly to endanger others, reward his actions, and encourage other wrongdoers to follow his example.

Love your enemy?

Love a Joseph Stalin? Love a Saddam Hussein? Love the man who murdered your father, the rapist who ravished your daughter? It would not only be impossible, it would be immoral.

WE NEED TO RE-EXAMINE some of the religious concepts we learned in childhood and relate them to our time. Jesus' teachings include many universal truths, applicable in any situation and in any century, but some of them are simply unsuited to our time. Why should one accept concepts appropriate to a Middle Eastern people thousands of years ago except as they travel well and are relevant in today's utterly different world?

There are profound insights in Judaism and Christianity, and one should count oneself fortunate for having been exposed to them from childhood. There can be no understanding our society, our laws, and our customs without a recognition of the formative contributions made to them by the Jews and by the Christian church, but it is a grievous error in judgement to hallow them and accept them today as the very Word of God.

The Bible contains the thoughts of men, not the Word of God, and we should approach it as we approach other extraordinary insights.

THE IDEA OF THE Bible's divine authorship abandoned, one is able to accept or reject or adapt its teachings to our time. Contemporary ethical questions can be examined on their merit without trying to make them conform to an ancient world-view. We are free to look at life without preconceptions and welcome what we find to be true, even when it runs counter to the teaching of the Bible or the church.

It is the vanity of most of us to believe that the concepts we were born to and the way we were raised are superior to other people's. But wisdom was not born with us and does not dwell with us. If our society has enshrined any fundamental truths, it is almost certain that the same principles have been ascertained by other civilized people. The basic societal concepts are not many and most modern nations have learned them, *had* to learn them in order to live in peace and perpetuate themselves. We and they may state them differently, call them by different names, observe them in different ways, and celebrate them differently, but the essential truths are the same wherever civilized men and women have joined to form societies.

For countless centuries the roles of men and women were determined by the customs of the world into which they were born and by the need to survive in hostile surroundings. Men controlled the home and the society. Women were regarded as inferior, often treated as little more than chattels. They had virtually no say in governing the community and were, in fact, a particular kind of slave. But as societies progressed they came to comprehend that all of us have certain basic birthrights: the right to life, to freedom, and to an opportunity to develop as we choose – all of this contingent, of course, on each individual respecting the right of others to do the same.

In modern times, most peoples and nations agree to codify such rights and to protect them from disrespect. In much of the Western world we have a largely Judeo-Christian tradition and our laws have been formulated by consensus within that context. Others, in other parts of the world, raised differently, see some things differently, but we are all kin beneath the skin and are slowly – oh, so painfully slowly! – coming to understand this.

The Illusion That
God Answers Prayer

With a contemporary understanding of how the universe came into being, knowing something about the universality of the laws that govern life, knowing that the God of the Bible is no more than a tribal god, knowing something of Jesus' despairing and unanswered prayer in the Garden of Gethsemane – "Father, if it be possible, let this cup pass from me" – does it make sense to get down on one's knees and ask God to intervene in one's life?

I had lunch recently with a young man, a stranger who had contacted me because of an interest in one of my books. He had been raised in a deeply religious family and was working on a doctorate in philosophy at the University of Toronto. In the midst of the meal he leaned across the table and, with a touch of impatience in his voice, asked, "How can anyone, at this point in history, get down on his knees and presume to ask the God of the universe to intervene personally on his behalf, to do what he – the guy doing the praying – wants? This isn't the Middle Ages. We know that we live in a universe controlled by immutable law. Knowing this, is there is any point in praying?"

He looked at me with a sly smile: "And beyond that, isn't it psychologically unhealthy to run to God with your problems, to slough off on him responsibilities which, in many cases, ought to be faced up to and dealt with as best one can?"

After a moment he continued: "Why am I asking you this? It's my upbringing. I learned to pray, as the saying has it, at my mother's knee, and even though I know it's pointless, I still find myself disposed to ask God's help on, say, the eve of a final or when I very much want something that seems out of reach or when I've got myself in some kind of serious trouble."

I began my response by telling him that his question reminded me of a story I once heard about a little boy who was asked if he said his prayers every night. He answered, "No, not every night. There's some nights I don't want nothin'."

FOR MOST OF US THE disposition to pray is almost instinctive. We face problems beyond our wisdom or our power to solve: a family member is ill; we very much want to achieve something apparently beyond our reach; we have pyramiding money problems; there are rumours that the company we work for is in serious financial straits and may go belly-up; tomorrow the doctor will give us the result of the tests he took the previous week . . .

When life is serene, when all is going reasonably well, we may not remember to pray, but when troubles encircle us and we reach the end of our tether, even the religiously indifferent may fashion a silent prayer. It has been said that,

> When the Devil is sick,
> The Devil a saint would be.

The astonishing thing is that earnest Christians continue to beseech God daily for things they want or for the resolution of problems they face despite the evident fact that few if any of their prayers are answered. It is common practice when praying to add the tag line, "If it be thy will" – this being, of course, the pious thing to say. But it is also a convenient device to enable the person praying to avoid the question: "I wonder if God really *does* answer prayer?"

A MORE PERTINENT question might be: What if everyone's prayers *were* answered? Consider for a moment the compounding chaos that could result if events on earth were controlled by any earnest Christian who bent his knee or bowed his head!

- What would happen in wartime when equally virtuous Christians on both sides are praying for victory?
- What would happen if the answer to your prayer would conflict with the best interests of other equally earnest people?
- What would happen in a football game between two Christian colleges when both teams bow their heads in the dressing room before the game and pray for victory?
- What would happen on a midsummer weekend when picnickers pray for sunshine, a bride prays for a perfect day for her wedding, a pastor prays for good weather for the annual children's picnic, and one hundred local farmers hold a twenty-four-hour prayer vigil to ask God to end a month-long drought?

If all our prayers were answered affirmatively, would it not mean that God had abdicated and that we were running the universe on an *ad hoc* basis? And when one considers the state of the world we *have* fashioned – the enmities and wars between nations and groups; the pollution of the atmosphere; the depletion of the ozone layer; the fouling of our lakes and rivers; the extinction of hundreds of species of animals and birds; the deforestation of the timberlands; the disparities between rich and poor; the grinding poverty of the slums; the crime in our streets; the scourge of the traffic in drugs; the accelerating world-wide death toll resulting from AIDS; the depletion of our fish stocks . . . the list is endless – one shudders to think of the consequences if we *were* running the universe through our prayers!

And beyond all this, is it not ridiculous to believe that the importunities of one individual or group of pious Christians would be required to persuade a loving and omniscient God to do something he would not otherwise do?

THE CHRISTIAN BELIEF that God answers prayer raises even more complex questions. If God can be convinced by one person to alter events, this means that the course of history can be radically changed by an individual on his knees.

Any change has ramifications. Any effect causes other effects, and once begun there may be no end to the forces set in motion; some of them possibly cataclysmic.

According to Christian theology, God is omniscient and exists apart from time. Being omniscient, he knows the end from the beginning. But, if true, would this not mean that all temporal life is predetermined. If God knows the end from the beginning then nothing is subject to change – otherwise, it could not have been known from the beginning.

This being so, prayer cannot possibly change anything and there is no point to it. Apart from its function as worship, prayer is based on the premise that God can be talked into running the universe according to the wishes of a devout person on his knees. But, again, try to imagine the chaos if every devout person's prayers *were* answered!

Belief in the efficacy of prayer is a form of self-delusion. Our real prayers are not what we say while on our knees – the facile words whispered during a prayer. They are the aspirations, attitudes, and desires that motivate our daily lives. It is easy to prime the pump and have the words gush forth in a torrent of pious phrases but the proof of what we really want – regardless of what we *say* we want – is evident in the way we live.

An individual's daily life is an unspoken prayer and is evidence of what the supplicant *really* wants. Many an individual prays for the strength of will to overcome a particular weakness and then puts himself in the way of temptation. Many pray for success but won't put in the hours and effort that success in any field requires. Many a father prays for his children's well-being but won't spend quality time with them. Many a student prays for straight A's but won't hit the books.

Despite protestations to the contrary, what we really want is usually evident to the astute observer. We reveal in our daily lives what our deepest desires are. Our true prayers are the way we live.

A World in Transition

*O*ur contemporary world would be unrecognizable to someone who lived and died as recently as the turn of the century.

Changes in transportation, communication, architecture, education, housing, entertainment, and clothing – not to mention attitudes and approaches to life – have made the present generation radically and dramatically different from all its predecessors.

Families used to live in the same house for generations. Today, one in every six North Americans moves his place of residence every ten years. Our homes are comfortable and convenient in ways previously undreamed of, but we spend less time in them.

We are different in our work.

The workplace has changed. The human hand has been outmoded by modern tools, by automation, and by the computer. Strength is no longer requisite; a woman can operate a great machine as well as a man. But so much work today is repetitious and requires so little creative involvement that many men and women are little more than an extension of a machine or mere scrutineers on an assembly line.

We are different in our amusements.

We are afflicted with "spectatoritis" – non-participation with others in our leisure time – and this has produced the so-called couch potato. The television set in the home, the proliferation of books and magazines, the giant screen in the theatres and mass spectator sports – where for every active participant there are a thousand watching –

provide most of our entertainment. And for the first time in history, amusements throughout the world are similar and often identical.

We are different in our education.

We are sometimes shocked by what people read, failing to be surprised that they read at all. It has not always been so: the barber's pole and the apothecary's jar are reminders of a day not long ago when a largely illiterate population recognized places of business by visual representations rather than words. Because of education, radio, television, motion pictures, computers, and the printing-press, the average citizen knows more about the world than his grandparents dreamed of.

We are different in the ways we communicate.

Handwriting is disappearing. So are typewriters. So is pen-in-hand personal correspondence – why scribble what you have to say when you can transmit it better and more speedily using a telephone, a computer, or a fax machine? There is also a diminution in close personal relationships, discussion groups, and churchgoing. It would appear that, to most, these don't seem as imperative or as important as they used to be.

BEYOND THESE CHANGES one can also perceive what appears to be a fundamental perversity in humankind that causes our best intentions to go awry:

- We fashion the miracle of flight only to load the wings with destruction.
- We transform the world into a neighbourhood and then make our proximity a threat to our existence.
- We design our communication systems to span the globe only to have them become instruments of propaganda.
- We probe to the heart of the atom only to use the power resident there to reduce our fellows to atoms.
- We build printing-presses with which to put good books within the reach of everyone and then build bigger presses to flood the bookstores and newsstands with intellectual junk food and pornography.

- We have television and motion pictures to provide information and recreation and we crowd the screen with low comedy and bloody it with violence and crime.
- We manufacture automobiles to provide faster and more comfortable transportation only to waste hours every day in traffic jams.
- We create miraculous medications to cure a host of diseases that once meant certain death, only to encounter new diseases and find that mental illness has become epidemic.
- We build supermarkets to make everything edible conveniently available, only to become a generation in which gross obesity is a commonplace and a major cause of early death.

AND WHERE IN THIS radically different world is the Christian church?

At the turn of the century the Christian church rested at the heart of the community. Attendance on a Sunday morning was *de rigueur* and in many churches the evening service was as popular as the morning. Many social events took place at the church. So did most funerals and all weddings. The Parson was "the person" in the community and it was almost obligatory for politicians to be seen in church on a Sunday morning.

Today, the impress of the church on our society is shallow. It remains a cherished institution but has little influence on the thinking or actions of most of its members. One's religion tends to exist apart from one's daily responsibilities. It does not move easily from the pew to the marketplace.

The average church member has little grasp of the meaning of the faith he or she espouses. We are innately religious but religiously illiterate. Many a church member matures in every area of life except the sacred, continuing to hold the outdated concepts about the nature and will of God, the Bible, and personal and corporate morality learned in Sunday school.

One's religion is, today, often more an inheritance than a choice – witness the man who says, "Our family has *always* been Baptist," or the woman who says, "I was born a Roman Catholic; I'll die a Roman Catholic."

The average Presbyterian might have considerable difficulty explaining why he is a Presbyterian rather than an Anglican and even more difficulty explaining just what he means on a Sunday morning when he repeats: "I believe in the Holy Ghost, the Holy Catholic Church, the communion of saints, the resurrection of the body, the forgiveness of sins, and the life everlasting."

THE CONTEMPORARY MEN and women to whom the church must address itself are increasingly complex creatures. Our minds are cluttered with snippets and patches of information – a veritable hodge-podge of ten thousand ill-understood ideas. And we are brainwashed daily with concepts born on Broadway or Hollywood and Vine, or on the other side of the world.

We are raised in a climate of self-expression but seldom pause to wonder whether we have a self worth expressing. We fear old age and struggle desperately to remain young – maturity aping youth and afraid to smile lest it betray a wrinkle. We worship youth, beauty, success, wealth, athletic proficiency, and the idealized female form. We fear death and use cosmetics to make our dead appear to be in the bloom of health. We want fitness without discipline, peace without involvement, religion without sacrifice, and sex without commitment.

Our generation seems to have found all the answers, except the important ones, namely, how to live with others and with ourselves. No other people in history have had so many benefits and conveniences and so many problems, and the Christian church – which was once the balance-wheel in society, the centre rather than the circumference – is becoming increasingly irrelevant.

One is reminded of William Butler Yeats's lines:

> Things fall apart, the centre cannot hold;
> Mere anarchy is loosed upon the world,
> . . .
> The best lack all conviction, while the worst
> Are full of passionate intensity.

The Myth of the Holy Trinity

The Christian Church teaches that there is one God.

Paradoxically, it also teaches that God is three persons – the Father, the Son, and the Holy Ghost – and that they are not mere manifestations of the deity. The Father is God, the Son is God, and so is the Holy Ghost. And they are co-eternal, co-equal, and co-existent.

Each, we are told, exists as an individual "person" but all three are "one God." As the familiar hymn puts it: "God in three persons; blessed Trinity."

But the concept will not bear examination. Matthew's Gospel tells us that before Mary of Nazareth became pregnant with the infant Jesus, the angel Gabriel appeared to the troubled Joseph – to whom she was betrothed – and told him not to be concerned, that "that which is conceived in her is of the Holy Ghost."

But the logic here is difficult to follow: If Jesus of Nazareth was, as the Christian church asserts, the Second Person of the Holy Trinity, he was "begotten" by a member of his own family, the Holy Ghost.

Moreover, the purported facts of Jesus' birth seem to indicate that the members of the Holy Trinity are not, as the Apostle's Creed states, co-equal and co-eternal. The Father, for instance, is unmistakably senior. He is the creator, the law-giver, and the prime mover, and the Son and the Holy Ghost are subject to him and do his bidding. It is he who directs the Holy Ghost to impregnate Mary – apparently with no reference to the Son – and he who has a voice from Heaven announce at Jesus baptism, "This is my beloved Son, in whom I am well pleased."

Jesus invariably addresses the First Person of the Holy Trinity as "Father" and is clearly subject to his authority. As John 3:16-17 states: "God so loved the world that he . . . sent his son into the world that the world might be saved through him." During his years on earth, the Son looked to the Father daily for guidance and wisdom. In difficult times, such as during his agony in the Garden of Gethsemane, the Son even pleads with the Father to be relieved of his assignment: "Father, if it be possible, let this cup pass from me," but makes it evident that he is subject to the Father by adding, "Nevertheless, not my will but thine be done." In the agony of the crucifixion he seems momentarily to doubt the Father's loyalty, addressing him as his God and crying out, "My God. My God, why have you forsaken me?"

There is another incongruity: If Jesus is, in fact, co-equal and co-eternal with the Father, why is he not mentioned in the Old Testament? There is not even an indirect reference to him. Nor is there any mention of him during the Creation. He played no part during Israel's captivity in Egypt nor in the miraculous escape when the Red Sea was parted, not even during the difficult years when the Israelites wandered in the wilderness. Nor was he present during the preparation of the Ten Commandments on Sinai – which, incidentally, he later reduced to one – or during the bloody conquest of the Promised Land. Where was God the Son through all those centuries and what was his role before the Nativity?

Who can blame the Jews for not recognizing him as their God? He played no part in Israel's history.

IN EVALUATING THE Christian concept of the Trinity, the reader can either accept by faith the claims of Jesus' divinity made by the Christian church or recognize the Nativity story for what it is – an invention of early Christians who came to believe that Jesus was divine and sought to validate their claim by insisting that he was the Son of God.

The Inquisition

*M*any think of the church as a sacred institution and of priests and the clergy as men wholly dedicated to the service of God and humankind. This assumption has not always been valid; indeed, it has seldom been so. In the Middle Ages, in particular, the Christian church approximated a terrorist organization, being the instigator and the protagonist in the indescribable horrors of the infamous Inquisition.

In France and, later, in other parts of Europe, beginning in the fourteenth century and peaking in the sixteenth and seventeenth centuries, tens of thousands of innocent men and women – even children – were persecuted, arrested, imprisoned, tried in secret, tortured, flayed, hanged, or burned at the stake in a protracted obsession with heretics, witches, sorcerers, black magic, and demon-possession.

As the influence and power of the Roman church spread in Europe and beyond, it denounced and, where it could, banned what it considered (sometimes justifiably) pagan beliefs and practices, which were common at that time. The specific goal of the Inquisition was the suppression of heresy and the conversion of a preponderance of all the nations of Europe to Roman Catholicism. The church was intractable in its opposition to anything it regarded as a deviant belief.

Those accused were given an opportunity to recant and, if they failed to do so, were brought to trial. Defendants were not given the names of their accusers and had no right to counsel. The trials were held behind closed doors but with a stipulated number of local laymen present. Torture of the accused and of his defence witnesses became customary. Most trials ended in a guilty verdict, resulting in the confiscation of the property of the accused which was then divided between the town and the church.

However, rather than repress superstition, the Inquisition actually stimulated belief in the occult, leading at times to mass hysteria.

Early in the fourteenth century, the number of prosecutions, trials, and convictions of accused witches increased greatly. Toward the end of the fifteenth century, Pope Innocent VIII issued a bull (proclamation) directing inquisitors to be even more vigilant in seeking out malefactors. This, of course, heightened the zeal of the authorities, the clergy, and the public, and their activities reached a peak during the sixteenth and seventeenth centuries. Under the authority of the Spanish Inquisition – which was conducted mostly by the government but with the consent of the church – as many as a hundred persons were burned as witches in a single day. In Geneva, Protestants joined the mass frenzy and, in one three-month period, burned no fewer than five hundred "witches."

These *autos-da-fé* – as public immolations came to be called – often took on the atmosphere of a carnival. People would gather, meet friends, buy souvenirs, rosaries, holy images of the saints and the Saviour, even food and drink, as they watched with apparent fascination the horrors taking place, usually in the town or city centre.

In the general hysteria and fanaticism of that era anyone might become suspect. Nor was it difficult to make a case for the existence of witches – segments of the Bible supplied the requisite data. Had not the Witch of Endor called up Samuel's body? Moreover, advocates of the burnings and other persecutions found validation for their activities in a proof-text straight from the scriptures: "Thou shalt not suffer a witch to live."

In England, where the Inquisition had less influence, a man was nonetheless burned at the stake for causing a storm at sea, his objective being, it was charged, to drown a member of the royal family. A woman was tried, convicted, and publicly burned for causing children to vomit crooked pins. One woman was found guilty of turning her-self into a fox. Others were accused of causing frost in summer, of destroying crops with hail, of making cows go dry, of souring beer . . .

At Vail in 1470, a rooster was charged with laying an egg. Members of the clergy solemnly swore that this was entirely likely: were not rooster eggs required in making witch-ointment? The rooster was found guilty and, with all due solemnity, burned in the town square.

Few of those charged were cleared. Women were torn from their husbands and children. Malice or harboured resentments were often the reasons for the laying of charges. Accusations of witchcraft and demon-possession became a means for taking revenge on an enemy or a way to confiscate an estate. Anyone might be accused – a wife, a husband, a neighbour, a child, an acquaintance – anyone who broke the normal pattern of life in the community or drew suspicion or merely had enemies in high places. To win confessions, the accused were tortured – three times if they were obdurate, this practice giving birth to the term "the third degree." The thumbscrew was frequently used to induce confessions as was an ingenious device that was inserted into the womb and expanded. As one might expect, most of the accused confessed – which, of course, only confirmed the belief in witches and evil spirits.

The horrors inflicted on dissidents or nonconformists are beyond description or imagination. The frenzy even spread across the Atlantic to the American colonies. In Salem, Massachusetts, in 1692, twenty people were executed as witches.

Ironically, the Inquisition was good for the economy. The charges, trials, cross-building, and gallows preparation created employment for many – among them lawyers, judges, carpenters, law-enforcement officials, prison guards, and, of course, gravediggers.

All this barbarism and cruelty in the name of Jesus of Nazareth, the Holy Christian church, and a God of love.

The Man in the Pulpit

Priests and Preachers

*E*very week of the year for centuries, millions of men and women in various parts of the world have sat in ordered rows in every kind of sanctuary, fixed their eyes on the person standing before them in the pulpit, and said in effect: "Talk to us about God. Tell us the meaning and purpose of life."

It is perhaps the greatest missed opportunity in history.

Rather than being an exciting exploration of life's basic questions it is, more often than not, an hour of tedium.

Religion is the most fascinating of all subjects, mostly because the existence and nature of God and the destiny of the world and of humankind are the subject matter. Has anyone ever lived who has not felt – even if only briefly – an aspiration toward God or the fear of him? Is there any human drive, excluding sex, love, and ambition, that has so motivated men or so influenced history? Men and women in every age have longed for God, lived for him, died for him. Others have welcomed poverty and dedicated themselves to sacrificial living. Still others have persecuted, pillaged, tortured, and killed in God's name. What single influence in history has created more beauty, fostered more aspiration, and kindled more hate and hypocrisy than religion?

Unfortunately, when the proclamation of the Christian faith degenerates into little more than a duty, a social occasion, a weekly obligation, it becomes a bore. Many clergymen reflect this *ennui* in their atonal delivery and their dispassionate demeanour, their weekly obligation having induced a stultifying familiarity with the task. Many clergymen come to this: the requisite duties degenerate to rote, the once sacred acts become ritual, and the reverence becomes feigned.

MEN AND WOMEN HAVE always been and will always be insatiably curious about the meaning and purpose of life. Is there a God? What is he like? Is there life after death? Is there in another world a place of bliss and rejoicing and, conversely, a place of punishment? Are there in the world to come rewards for living a moral and unselfish life and suffering for the failure to do so?

Across the centuries millions have turned to the clergy hoping, if not necessarily to get final answers, at least to get valid insights into the eternal.

Most of the time, it has been a vain hope.

During my more than twenty years in the ministry I came to know many clergymen. These "men of the cloth" were as varied as the elaborately gowned archbishop, the minister of the local church, the homespun country pastor, the Salvation Army officer, the ecstatic Pentecostal, the money-grubbing television evangelist, and others.

What kind of men – and only occasionally women – are these "men of God"?

Simply put, no different from other men and women; no better, no worse. I have known clergymen who come as close as men do to saintliness and some who were, in a word, corrupt. Decent men, by and large, the majority are no more moral or intelligent or insightful or altruistic or reverent than their counterparts in the pews.

Clergymen are given automatic respect by virtue of their vocation. They are, of course, no more deserving of this than men in other professions. Many of them are intellectually limited men with closed minds, hidebound in their thinking and set in their views. Many are compassionate, concerned, at ease with strangers. Some are pompous, typically introducing themselves with "I'm the Reverend John Smith," apparently unaware that the word is first of all an adjective meaning holy, and certainly not a title. Some are cloying and a shade precious. I heard it said of a preacher of my acquaintance: "He's a good brother; he's also a good sister."

Clergymen tend to be – as befits their calling – gregarious. A few – surprisingly, because they live much of their life in public – are ill at ease in social intercourse. Fortunately, in the pulpit, they lose the self-consciousness so evident in informal situations.

It has been my observation that most intelligent clergymen preach to the right of their theology; they are more conservative in the pulpit than they are in private conversation or when counselling a parishioner. It is difficult if not impossible for an intelligent man to accept the Bible as "the very Word of God." Clergymen know better than most that it is not a sacred relic handed down intact from Heaven.

If the clergyman is an intelligent man he knows that much in the Bible is incompatible with contemporary knowledge. He knows also that the unimaginable immensity of the universe and the variety and complexity of human life cannot be reduced to dogma. He is aware of the paradoxes – life's ineffable beauty and its too frequent horrors – and if he is an honourable man is hesitant to proffer pat little panaceas as solutions to the complex problems of modern life – of which, because of his calling, he sees more than most.

The intelligent clergyman will almost invariably end up turning a blind eye to the contradictions and implausibilities in the Bible and the sometimes totalitarian attitudes of the Church. He simply sets them aside. It is not a reprehensible hypocrisy. The rationale is that there is so much that is good in the Christian tradition – especially in the life and teaching of Jesus of Nazareth – that much if not most of the Gospel can in good conscience be proclaimed with conviction.

With the years he will increasingly eschew the dogmatic and may, as his early passion cools, end up bored and something of a bore. In the end he is likely to settle for what might best be described as an altruistic do-goodist Christian philosophy.

THE FUNDAMENTALIST clergy are a breed apart. They tend to be zealous, unsophisticated men and women. Fundamentalists are great "believers," prepared to accept without question the most outrageous concepts. They assert – and a majority believe – that the Bible is the inerrant, infallible Word of God and they accept every word in it as literal truth. They believe in a personal Devil, "who goes about seeking whom he may devour," that Adam and Eve were real people, created by the hand of God in an earthly paradise called the Garden of Eden, and that their eating of the forbidden fruit – commonly thought of as an apple – left all men sinners by nature. They believe in a literal Heaven and an everlasting fire-and-brimstone Hell where all those who have not "accepted Jesus Christ as their personal Saviour" will be tormented forever. They believe that Almighty God selected one small nation, Israel, as his Chosen People and, for their exclusive guidance, inscribed the Ten Commandments on tablets of stone. They believe that a Palestinian virgin was impregnated by God the Holy Ghost, that her son, Jesus of Nazareth, was God in the flesh, that he was executed by the Roman government but was resurrected by God the Father, that he ascended into Heaven and will return to earth some day soon to judge the 5.6 billion living humans and consign the wicked to endless torment.

A MAJOR FACTOR IN the dramatic decrease in attendance at church services around the world is undoubtedly the irrelevance of contemporary preaching. There are few gifted preachers today. Men who can seize and hold the attention of an audience with their words are in demand and usually feel called by God to accept pulpits in the larger, more prosperous churches.

The common characteristics of most clergymen are conservatism and dullness. Dullness in the pulpit is a greater disservice to a congregation than faulty exegesis or shoddy homiletics. It is incredible that so much contemporary preaching is boring. That the Christian message should bore anyone is itself astonishing. The Old Testament is replete with high drama and tenanted by wonderfully colourful characters. Jesus' teachings in the New Testament speak to the fundamental moral and ethical issues of our time, and his life presents as a challenge the superlative exemplar in Western history. Yet, somehow, many if not most preachers manage to transform the transforming message of the Gospel into the pallid, innocuous moralism that proceeds from so many pulpits today.

It is no easy thing to make the Christian story boring, and it could

not be done if the preacher were not able to borrow from a long tradition of dullness.

THERE ARE FEW opportunities for influence comparable to that
afforded the Christian minister. He is free to choose his subject and,
uninterrupted, press his convictions on his hearers. Every week, clergymen around the world have a captive audience of millions of men and
women seated before them and ready to give ear to what they have to
say. What other cause has a comparable forum? That the average
Christian is so untutored in his faith and so ineffective as a moral
influence in the society makes it obvious that the opportunity is
largely wasted.

It may be, as was mentioned earlier, the greatest missed opportunity in history.

One reason for this failure is that many preachers try to popularize the teachings of Jesus. Those who do have forgotten the warning
of Isaiah: "These are a rebellious people who will not hear the instruc-
tion of the Lord: who say to the prophets, 'Preach not to us what is
right, speak to us smooth things.' "

Jesus did not instruct his disciples to popularize the Gospel but to
proclaim it. That it is impossible to preach the Christian Gospel fully
and not be unpopular in some quarter is surely evident when one
remembers what happened to the one who originated the message. In
the early months of his ministry, Jesus was greeted with wild adulation. But when they heard him out, the sky darkened, the cheers
turned to murmurings, and ended with the cry, "Crucify him!"

Jesus said to his hearers: "Let him who would come after me, take
up his cross and follow me." This was no invitation to a Sunday-
school picnic. To transpose his invitation to contemporary argot, it is
as though he was saying to the five thousand he had fed with the
loaves and fishes: "Look! You who enjoyed the free lunch should
understand from the beginning that this is not an invitation to play
Church."

But this is not the emphasis one commonly hears today. You are
more likely to hear sinewless musing about "The Goal Is Goodness"

or "The Darkness of Doubt" – two sermon subjects drawn from a recent Sunday church page in the *Toronto Star*.

But "where the trumpet is needed the flute will not suffice."

One flinches at the memory of hearing in a wealthy New York City church the Almighty God addressed in prayer as though he was "one of the boys," someone with whom the preacher was on terms of buddy-buddy intimacy. This reverend gentleman, this gregarious man-among-men, seemed almost driven to demonstrate that, for all the fact he was a clergyman, he was "with it" and tuned to the twentieth century.

He is representative of too many who substitute *bonhomie* for caring.

At the opposite extreme is the philosopher-priest. He is much given to quoting esoteric sources and current philosophical wisdom and invariably manages in the twenty-or-so minutes allowed him to convey, albeit obliquely, the breadth of his scholarship.

The desire in a preacher for intellectual respectability is a snare. Some sermons are so studded with learned quotes and literary allusions that they are not so much sermons as essays and sound as though they have been written with *Bartlett's Familiar Quotations* at one hand and *Roget's Thesaurus* at the other.

Then there are the borrowers: preachers who proclaim what has been called "a gossip theology," snippets and patches from the printed sermons of others, pasted together in a pulpit pastiche.

Thomas Merton relates, in his book *The Seven Story Mountain*, how, as a young student, in an agony of spiritual confusion and hungering for a crumb of certitude, he frequently attended a popular Protestant church in New York City:

> The minister of the church was very friendly and used to get into conversations about modern literature and intellectual matters – even men like D.H. Lawrence with whom he was thoroughly familiar. He seemed to count very much on that sort of thing; considered it an essential part of his ministry. That was precisely one of the things that made the experience of going to his church such a sterile one for me. It was modern literature and politics that he talked about; not religion and

God. You felt that the man did not know his vocation, did not know what he was supposed to be.

Fundamentalists, at the other extreme, major in passion. They are much given to elitist talk about their personal relationship to God and tend to be judgemental and distrustful of other Christians. Informality is the norm in their services. Decorum is dispensed with and self-expression to the point of incoherence is often interpreted as evidence that the Holy Ghost has taken over.

The Pentecostal clergy are much given to "speaking in tongues." They take literally the scripture verse: "and they all spake with other tongues as the Spirit gave them utterance." To see a congregation of fervent Pentecostals beseeching God to "cast out the Devil" from one in their midst is to see the dictionary definition of fanaticism embodied.

This is not to charge a lack of sincerity – the fundamentalists are as much interested in letting God into their lives as are the earnest worshippers whispering their ritual prayer in a cathedral – it is simply that they are, culturally, different kinds of people.

It should be noted that the Pentecostal church is the fastest-growing denomination in Christendom. It is adding to its numbers while the traditional communions are losing worshippers at a rate which, if continued for another two or at most three generations, will leave them a relic.

There is, however, little likelihood that the fundamentalists will become a major influence in Western society. Their members are mostly working men and women – earnest, zealous, and well-intentioned – but their simplistic theology and their essentially emotional response to public worship limit their opportunity.

BY WAY OF CONTRAST: I recently visited a Sunday-morning service in a prestigious, long-established Protestant church in downtown Toronto. The pews were no more than one-third filled. There were many more women than men present, a majority of them middle-aged or older. There was an evident scarcity of young people. The central figure on the stained-glass window – an image of Jesus – looked like an impassive ascetic.

The principal prayer, although addressed to God, was aimed at the people. Most of the prayer was spent informing God about things one would presume he knew. The sermon, delivered by a man garbed entirely in black – that least appropriate of Christian colours – was a rambling, uninspiring, ill-organized homily on one's moral obligations to others. It was pretty innocuous stuff, only peripherally Christian, and seemed neither to comfort nor to challenge anyone. There was no passion, nothing to stir the blood or set the heart to singing.

Had Jesus been in the pulpit that Sunday morning there can be little doubt that he would have scandalized that congregation, as he did those who gathered to hear him in the synagogues and in the streets of Jerusalem two thousand years ago. When Jesus concluded his maiden sermon in his home town, they tried to pitch him off a cliff.

I neither saw nor heard anything to remind me of the Jesus of the Gospels on that sunny Sunday morning in downtown Toronto.

BUT AT LEAST THERE was some rationality in what the reverend gentleman said. The following Sunday I turned on my television set to watch a renowned evangelist and sat astonished that such transparent flimflammery could successfully masquerade as Christianity.

Fundamentalist television evangelism is a twentieth-century Christian heresy. It is part show business, part pious claptrap, and as unlike New Testament Christianity as a newspaper horoscope. It is a mediapostasy that tells listeners all they have to do to become Christians is to "believe." As I listened to the evangelist hammer home his threadbare theme again and again, I also heard echoing in my memory the voice of the apostle James saying: "You believe there is one God; you do well. The devils also believe – and tremble!"

Modern television evangelists are mostly ignorant men with closed minds who have glimpsed the incredible reach of television – even its political influence – and spend a sizable part of their air time pleading for money.

The most unsavoury among the television clergy are undoubtedly the healing evangelists. Most of them are so patently kooks that one watches them with that awed fascination once reserved for freaks in county fairs. They are quacks, practising spiritual medicine without a licence, offering remedies they neither understand nor have troubled to examine. They are not sufficiently intelligent to be truly evil but are nonetheless harmful, leaving in their wake a pathetic trail of emotional wreckage and, oftentimes, illnesses worsened by the failure to get medical treatment. And for all their claims, they effect few – if any – valid cures.

One of the most reprehensible things about these exploiters of the gullible is that they mulct their millions mostly from the poor, the elderly, and lonely middle-aged women. They trumpet the good they do but relatively few of the dollars put in their bottomless begging-bowls are used to give succour to the needy, put food in empty bellies, or help the helpless and the dispossessed. Most of it goes to buy more broadcast time, build greater facilities, and provide generous incomes, lavish homes, and high living for "the man of God."

Jesus reserved his harshest judgement for those who professed to be righteous but failed to feed the hungry, clothe the poor, visit the sick and imprisoned. "Depart from me, you accursed!" he thundered.

As I watched this particular exploiter of the gullible I could not help but wonder: If Jesus were here on earth would he make a guest appearance on one of his shows? Or would he fashion a whip out of television cables and drive the man from his microphone?

EVEN THE OLDEST AND largest of the Christian communions, the Roman Catholic church, has lost touch with the Jesus of the New Testament.

A single example: Not long ago the combined might of Pope John Paul II, the Vatican, and the National Council of Catholic Bishops in the United States joined together to condemn one of their own, Seattle's Archbishop Raymond Hunthausen, and to strip him of much of his ecclesiastical authority.

His sin? He had permitted a group of Catholic homosexuals to participate in the Mass in his cathedral. Moreover, it was charged, he was soft on divorce and on the rigid observance of sacramental rules.

A Vatican spokesman justified the church's action with an astounding statement: "No business would stand for a daughter concern that so openly drifted from company policy." (The church is a *business*?) By any reach of the imagination does that sound like the authentic voice of Jesus? It is the sound of an authoritarian organization guarding its temporal power.

Surely the question requires to be asked: If, as the church insists, homosexual behaviour is sinful – and the Bible teaches that it is – why may *these* sinners not come with other sinners to the altar?

Can one imagine Jesus turning them away? Hardly, when one remembers the consideration he showed the woman caught in the act of adultery. The religious leaders of that time – Pharisees, they were called – wanted to turn that "whore" away when she sought forgiveness. They wanted her stoned to death as the Old Testament prescribes. Jesus told them to go right ahead, but with one proviso: let the man who throws the first stone be someone who is himself free from sin.

How many priests are free from sin? Is the Pope himself free from sin? Are the archbishops? Are the clergy? Of course not. If they are, why do they each make their confession daily?

So what were these clerical sinners doing with rocks in their hands?

But to ask a more fundamental question: What is this enormous, multibillion-dollar hierarchical apparatus of richly attired popes, archbishops, bishops, foreign ministers, Vatican spokesmen, and on and on? Did not the founder of the Christian church say, "Everyone who exalts himself will be humbled"?

Who are these men who have taken a vow of poverty and teach that humility is a Christian virtue? What are they doing in their ornate cathedrals, attired in their costly raiment when Jesus told a man zealous to follow him, "Go sell what you possess and give it to the poor . . . *then* come follow me"? These men – and they are all men; no women allowed – sleep in marble palaces; their founder "had no place to lay his head."

And why do they insist on being called "Father" when Jesus, speaking of religious teachers, said specifically, "Call no man on earth your father, for you have one Father, who is in heaven."

Try to imagine what Jesus' reaction would be if he returned to earth, touched down at the Colonnade in Rome, and was taken on a tour of the opulent, multibillion-dollar magnificence of St. Peter's Cathedral, the exquisite Sistine Chapel, and the dozens of other elaborate and costly Vatican buildings – *and then be informed that it is a memorial to him!*

IF JESUS OF NAZARETH were here on earth, would he call himself a Christian? He might, because of such as the Mother Teresas of the world. Or because of men like an anonymous group of Mennonites who turned up early one morning in Barrie, a small city north of Toronto, part of which had been devastated when a tornado touched down the day before. Carpentry tools in hand, they purchased the materials needed and repaired at no charge the damage done to the houses of aging women or women who were living alone or ill. Then, declining to be interviewed by the press and television, they left as unostentatiously as they had arrived.

I am sure, however, that he would not align himself with most of the standard-brand churches of today. What connection has the contemporary Christian church and much of the clergy to the Jesus of the New Testament? Increasingly, the various expressions of the church become removed from the spirit and teaching of their founder.

And, as a consequence, the church is dying.

A Tale of Two Preachers

This is the story of two preachers, both friends of mine in my early years in the ministry. I will call the first Bob, not his real name. The other is Arthur Chote.

I met Bob before I made the decision to become a Christian. I was eighteen and working at the Toronto *Globe and Mail*. It was the "Dirty Thirties," the nadir of the Great Depression. Our family – Mother, a younger brother, three sisters, and I – lived on the ground floor in a five-room duplex in the west end of Toronto.

One day, Mother informed us over our groans of protest that we were going to have as a house-guest a young preacher who was to be the evangelist for a two-week campaign at her church. This required my brother and me to surrender our bedroom and move out to a shed behind the house, where we slept on an old mattress on a concrete floor. Bob, his wife, and their infant child moved in. To my surprise, I was soon greatly impressed by him. He was a full-time itinerant evangelist who conducted fifteen-day campaigns in local churches. He was in his early thirties, lean, handsome, with dark wavy hair. He was always impeccably dressed and was a fascinating conversationalist with a wealth of stories about his experiences and travels.

To my great relief he didn't talk religion, other than to say to me occasionally: "Come hear me preach one night."

The others in the family did but I did not.

Early in the morning on the closing Sunday of the campaign he came to the door of the shed where I was still asleep and reminded me that it was his last day in Toronto. "C'mon, slugabed," he said. "Last chance."

He was dressed in a white suit, a red carnation in his lapel, and, with a dazzling morning sun behind him outlining his silhouette and making a halo of his hair, he looked, I thought, like a young god.

A year or so later I became an active Christian. My job as sports cartoonist at the *Globe and Mail* made me something of a minor celebrity and I was soon being invited to speak at young people's meetings in the Toronto area. I would set up my easel and, and with a large pad of drafting paper, coloured chalks, and special lighting, make swift sketches illustrating biblical themes as I spoke.

Not long afterward, Bob returned to Toronto for a Sunday at our church. He was on his way to conduct a two-week campaign in North Tonawanda, New York, and urged me to join him. "You'll lead the singing," he said, "and do a drawing each night. It will help get young people out to the meeting. And I'll pay you twenty-five dollars a week."

The money was tempting and so was the opportunity. I arranged for time off at the newspaper and went with him.

Bob's skill with words was extraordinary. The illustrations he used and the anecdotes he told gripped his audiences in a way I have seldom seen equalled. Each night, my responsibilities finished, I would sit utterly engrossed – moved at times – watching him. The audience grew nightly and soon overflowed the church. People sat in chairs placed in the aisles, young people sat on the floor at the base of the pulpit, and others stood in rows at the back of the sanctuary and in the doorways. On the closing night many were turned away at the doors.

AS WE LOADED OUR luggage and got into my car to take the road back to Toronto, Bob said, "Now, let's you and me have some fun."

Telling me nothing more, he directed me to drive a few miles toward Buffalo to a roadside restaurant where, as we pulled up in front, a woman was standing in a doorway. "I been waitin' a dog's age," she said crossly as she climbed into the back seat. Bob slipped out of his seat and joined her.

As he gave directions, I turned down a dark rural road. "In there," he said, pointing to a laneway. "Park in behind the barn."

Puzzled, trying to make sense out of what was happening, I did as I was told. There were no lights in the nearby house and the darkness was intense. But there was activity in the seat behind me, bodies moving, whispering and occasional giggling – and then the unmistakable sounds of lovemaking.

I sat in the darkness, completely at a loss. Not twenty minutes earlier we had been in the crowded church and Bob had led a prayer for the new converts.

Later, we dropped off the woman. Before I could say anything, he said, "Head into town."

In downtown Buffalo, he directed me to a street lined with scruffy stores. There were prostitutes standing in doorways or walking slowly back and forth on the sidewalk. "Lock your door," Bob said, "and pull up at the curb." He lowered his window and, as one of the women approached, bantered with her, asking for details of the services she was prepared to provide.

The woman grew impatient. "Let's get goin'," she said, and reached for the back door.

Bob shouted at me, "Take off!"

A few blocks down the street, he told me again to pull over to the curb. Two women approached. Again he detailed what he wanted, using the most explicit language. Suddenly angry, I put the car in gear, muttered something about "we've got to go," and pulled away from the curb.

We drove in silence, passed through customs at the border, and headed for Toronto. After a while, Bob began to talk, not with his usual fluency but haltingly, low-voiced, about how his wife abhorred sex. He followed this with a rambling explanation of his "weakness," as he called it. "Pray for me, Chuck," he said.

It took weeks to get the memory of that night out of the forefront of my mind.

I never saw Bob again. Some years later, when I had entered the ministry, I heard news about him from time to time. I learned that he had been ousted from a church for financial irregularities and other things and that he had moved from one pastorate to another, ending up in a small suburban church in the American South.

Bob was the most gifted preacher I have ever heard. As the saying has it: "He could bring Heaven down."

ARTHUR CHOTE ATTENDED the church where I was the minister in the 1940s, the Avenue Road Church in Toronto. He was a tall, lean man, two or three inches over six feet, and was studying theology at Wycliffe College at the University of Toronto preparatory to being ordained by the Anglican Church of Canada. I had noticed him in the congregation because of his height but we did not meet for a month or two. He introduced himself, somewhat shyly, one Sunday morning at the close of the service.

"I've been wondering what I can do to help," he said. "And I have a suggestion. I know how occupied you are, not just with the Sunday services but with the weekly broadcasts, the Saturday-night young people's rallies in Massey Hall, your outside speaking engagements, weddings, funerals, sermon preparation, sick visitation, and on and on. I'm told that there are some members of the church who are ill or handicapped and can't get out to the services. You can't possibly visit them all. Perhaps I could do some of this for you."

He went to work quietly, unobtrusively, reporting to me with brief notes rather than in person, "so that I won't take up your time." Once, he asked me to appeal to the congregation for unused portable radios so that the bedridden could listen to our broadcasts. A dozen or more were donated and he distributed and redistributed them to those who needed them. It is not possible to list the various behind-the-scenes kindnesses he dispensed, the errands he ran for the invalids, and the hospital patients he visited. Nor would he accept remuneration, not even gas for his car.

And during this period he was up to his ears in study, preparing for the Anglican priesthood.

The Second World War was at its height and Art came to me seeking counsel. He was a pacifist by conviction but, because of the scope of Hitler's depredations, felt compelled to volunteer for the armed services. I suggested that he take a week to think it through and then follow his convictions.

He joined the Royal Canadian Air Force. Within a year he had become an instructor, training recruits to fly twin-engine Anson bombers. He volunteered to go overseas but his senior officers felt he was too valuable in the training program.

I had some years earlier earned a private pilot's licence and one day he took me up in an Anson – as he said, to check out whether I had gotten rusty. In flight, he covered the canopy (as was done to teach night flying) and made me fly blind. And, of course, in the camaraderie of men, gave me a hard time.

Some years later he called one day to tell me that he was going to marry a woman he had met at our church and to ask if I would perform the ceremony. It was a happy occasion, with dozens of those for whom he had done kindnesses present.

After the war, when I left Toronto to study at Princeton, Art, now Canon Arthur Chote, was appointed rector of the Anglican church across the street from the church I had served and he had attended. Every time I returned home for a visit I heard stories of Art Chote's kindnesses. They were legion. Some years later, after a prolonged and painful illness, he died at Sunnybrook Hospital in Toronto – the finest example of a committed Christian I met during my twenty years in the ministry.

Two men, both preachers. One greatly gifted but morally corrupt. The other, the finest human being I have known.

Women

Women in the Bible

What is the status of women in the Bible?

Even a perfunctory reading makes it clear that, with rare exceptions, women were regarded and treated as inferior, subsidiary creatures, often as little more than chattels. When, as the Genesis account states, Yahweh decided to create humankind, he created a man who is described in the Eighth Psalm as "a little lower than the angels." The creation of the first woman was little more than a utilitarian afterthought. Yahweh said: "It is not good that the man should be alone; I will make him a help meet for him." He then proceeded to create not a woman, but the various animals, bringing them before Adam that he might name them. "But" as the text states, "for Adam there was not found an help meet for him." Yahweh then made woman, not creating her from dust, as he had Adam, but "took one of his ribs . . . made he a woman and brought her unto the man. And the rib which the Lord God had taken from the man he made into a woman."

THE BIBLE IS A BOOK by and for men. The women in it are secondary creatures and usually inferior. The woman is portrayed as the temptress in Eden, the tool of the serpent (a.k.a. Satan). He gulled her into getting her husband to eat of the forbidden fruit – "the fruit of the Tree of the Knowledge of Good and Evil." When, as a consequence of their disobedience, the first couple was banished from Eden, Yahweh laid a threefold curse on all women:

- That her suffering in childbearing would be "greatly multiplied."
- That she would nevertheless be made to lust for her husband.
- That she would be subsidiary to the man: "He will rule over
  you."

This superior/inferior relationship continued throughout the history of Israel. Women had little status and few rights. The Old
Testament is, with rare exceptions, the story of the exploits and
achievements of men. In most cases, when the lives of men and their
sons are chronicled, neither the man's wife nor the daughters that
issued from the marriage are so much as named.

It was, quite literally, a man's world.

THE GOD OF THE Bible is not genderless; he is male. His attributes
are masculine as are his actions and most of his attitudes. The Holy
Trinity comprises three males, the Father, the Son, and the Holy Ghost.
Jesus was himself unquestionably male, and when it became needful
that the Virgin Mary be impregnated so that he might be brought
into the world as a man, the Holy Ghost "came upon her" and Jesus
was conceived.

Adam and Eve had three children, all male: Cain, Abel, and Seth.
They may have had daughters but the writer of the Genesis account
does not find them worth mentioning. In the long list of Adam's
descendants over the hundreds of years that intervened before the
Great Flood, *not one female is so much as named!*

Noah was married but his wife's name is not given. He had three
married sons, Ham, Shem, and Japheth, but their wives are not
named. Only eight people went into the ark – Noah, his sons, and
their wives – but we do not know the name of any of the women; they
are merely the wives of the men. After the death of Noah the geneal-
ogy of his son's descendants is documented. Only sons are named.
Every marriage is noted but never once is the bride named.

Male pre-eminence ruled also in the satisfactions of the flesh.
Polygamy is permitted in the Old Testament and is covered by a number of statutes – but only for men! A man was free to have as many

wives and concubines as he could support. The great Jewish patriarchs, Abram, Moses, Joshua, and David all had more than one wife – Solomon, no fewer than seven hundred, not to mention three hundred concubines! – but no woman in Israel was permitted to have more than one husband.

A man could "put away" (divorce) his wife for any number of reasons but a woman could not separate from her husband except under the most extraordinary circumstances.

An unmarried woman was regarded as the property of her father or of a brother. A father could, at his option, give her away or, indeed, sell her to a prospective husband. He could also sell her as a slave and she had no say in the transaction. A prospective groom paid what was called a "bride price," in part because the bride had some value around the house and in the bedroom and because if she bore him children they would be the property of the husband. If a man seduced a virgin he was required to pay her father a bride price and do so even if the father refused to give her to the seducer in marriage.

Married, the woman remained a chattel. If her husband died before she bore him a son she was not permitted to marry anyone outside the family. Her husband's brother was required to take her as his wife and the first-born son of that marriage bore the name of the dead husband.

A man could offer his daughter as a prize. King Saul offered his eldest daughter to the man who would bring down Goliath, and his youngest daughter to the man who would bring him the foreskins of one hundred Philistines.

How's *that* for status!

Adultery was defined as "lying with another man's wife" and was viewed from the male perspective only. If a man committed adultery he was regarded as having transgressed, not against his wife, but against the husband of the woman with whom he had the illicit relationship.

The penalty for adultery was death for both the man and the woman. If a husband thought his wife had committed adultery and "if the spirit of jealousy came upon the husband," he could take her to a priest who would determine her guilt or innocence with a magic potion. She was required to drink the potion, and if she was guilty her thigh would swell up. If, however, she was found innocent, her husband was liable for any damages she suffered from the treatment.

THERE IS A PRIME example of the working of this double standard during Israel's many battles after coming out of the wilderness. Yahweh orders Moses to "execute his vengeance on Midian." Twelve thousand men are mustered. They attack the Midianites and kill every male. They then kill the five kings of Midian, and their children, seize as booty all their cattle, their flocks, their donkeys, and their possessions, burn all their cities and encampments to the ground, and take as bounty anything of value. But when the leaders of his army report to Moses on their victory he grows angry. "Why," he asks, "have you spared the lives of all the women? They were the ones," he reminds them, "who had perverted the sons of Israel." So he sends them back to finish the job, ordering that every male child and every woman who is not a virgin be killed. "Spare the lives of the young women, those who have not known a man by lying with him. Take them for yourselves."

The women of enemy nations were regarded as part of the spoils of war. The law of Israel specified: "When you go to war against your enemies and take prisoners: if you see a beautiful woman among the prisoners and find her desirable, you may make her your wife and bring her to your home. Should she cease to please you, you will let her go where she wishes, not selling her for money. You are not to make any profit out of her *since you have had the use of her*. [Italics mine]"

If a man married a woman and later turned against her, publicly defaming her by saying he had not found evidence of her virginity, he was required to take her before the elders and so state. Then, if the woman's parents could not produce evidence that she was indeed a virgin at the time of her marriage, she was taken to the door of her father's house and stoned to death.

A woman had no status even in a quarrel between her husband and another man: "When two men are fighting," the Mosaic law said, "if the wife of one intervenes by putting out her hand and seizing the other by the private parts, you shall cut off her hand and show no pity."

NOT ALL THE WOMEN in the Old Testament are ciphers. Some are portrayed as wise, courageous, and gifted. Indeed, two books of the Old Testament bear the names of women: Ruth and Esther. Ruth is of particular interest because, although she was a foreigner – a Moabite – she married a man from Bethlehem and, when he died, did not remain in Moab but returned to Bethlehem with her mother-in-law, Naomi. She eventually married one of Naomi's relatives and gave birth to a son who became King David's grandfather, and thus an ancestor of Jesus of Nazareth.

There were deceitful and wickedly seductive women in the Old Testament, women whose names still echo across the centuries. Among them, Potiphar's wife Delilah, who seduced Samson, and Jezebel, the wife of King Ahab and the bitter foe of Elijah, whose name remains synonymous with shamelessness and wickedness. Foreign women are usually suspect in the Old Testament, yet both of Moses' wives were gentiles and there are three foreign women in the line of David's ancestors.

It was a man's world. Yahweh almost exclusively conversed with, gave orders to, rewarded, punished, and often intervened personally on behalf of men.

ISRAEL'S ATTITUDE toward women is starkly and tragically revealed in the story, retold here in contemporary language, of Jephthah's daughter.

Jephthah, the son of Gilead, was a renowned warrior but he was a bastard child, his mother being a whore. Gilead's legitimate sons drove him from the family and from the town, and Jephthah, leading a group of misfits and malcontents, became a kind of soldier of fortune, living off the area by raiding and looting.

In the meantime, the Israelites were facing problems. They had been worshipping gods other than Yahweh and he had abandoned them. Under assault by a people called the Ammonites, and in desperate straits, the Israelites turned to Jephthah. "Come be our leader," they pleaded.

A deal is struck and Jephthah takes command. In a strategic move, he leads his troops to the rear of the Ammonite army. Just before the battle is joined, he makes a deal with God: "Deliver the Ammonites into my hands," he says to Yahweh, "and the first person who comes through the door of my house to greet me on my return shall belong to Yahweh. I will offer him up as a burnt offering."

Jephthah attacks and Yahweh delivers the Ammonites into his hands.

As he returns home, the first to greet him as he approaches his house is his daughter, who is celebrating his victory by dancing to the sound of a tambourine in her hands. When Jephthah sees her, he rips his clothes in his anguish and says to her, "Oh, my daughter, what sorrow you bring me! Must the cause of my ill fortune be you? I have made a vow to Yahweh and I cannot unsay what I have said."

She answers him, "My father, you have made a vow to Yahweh; treat me as you have vowed to do. But first, grant me one request: free me for two months to wander in the wilderness with some of my friends that I may bewail my virginity."

The two months pass and she returns to her father. Then, in the chilling words of the text: "He did with her what according to the vow he had pledged." In plain English: he offered her up to Yahweh as a human sacrifice. With his own hands he killed his daughter and burned her body on an altar, dedicating her to God.

And we are never so much as told her name!

Could there be a more tragic story, or one that more clearly reveals the male chauvinism and barbaric cruelty of the God of the Bible?

Even more shocking is the fact that Yahweh permits Jephthah to go through with it and then honours him for his commitment by making him a judge in Israel for the rest of his life!

The immolation of this young woman was not untypical of the way women were regarded in biblical times. Even their menstrual periods were seen as reprehensible.

She shall remain in her impurity for seven days. Everything she lies on or sits on shall be regarded as unclean. Whoever touches her clothes or her bed shall wash his clothes and bathe, but will remain unclean throughout the day. And if her period goes beyond seven days, she is to take two turtledoves and two young pigeons to the priest and the priest shall make atonement for her before the Lord for her unclean discharge.

SOLOMON WAS UNDOUBTEDLY one of Israel's most extraordinary kings. His wisdom was legendary. His devotion to Yahweh was, in most ways, exemplary. The temple he built for the worship of God was dazzling. Its furnishings were elaborate and expensive.

And Solomon's personal wealth was renowned. He sat on "a throne of ivory plated with refined gold." A single statement makes evident the opulence of his palace: "All of King Solomon's drinking vessels were gold, and all the furnishings in the Hall of the Forest of Lebanon were pure gold. *Silver was little thought of in the time of Solomon.* [Italics mine]"

Little wonder the Queen of Sheba travelled a great distance to meet him.

Equally extravagant was Solomon's love life. This servant of Yahweh, this king of Israel, this son of King David was a sex machine on a scale unequalled in recorded human history.

Let the text speak:

"He had seven hundred wives of royal rank and three hundred concubines. As well, King Solomon loved many foreign women; not only Pharaoh's daughter but Moabites, Edomites, Sidonians and Hittites." This, it should be noted, despite Yahweh's prohibition, "You are not to go to them or they to you."

And this led to trouble. His foreign wives pressured him into offering worship to other gods (Astarte was a favourite), and this, as might be expected, displeased Yahweh, by his own description of himself, a "jealous God." But he contained his displeasure and said to Solomon, "Since you do not keep my covenant or the laws I laid down for you, I will tear the kingdom from you and give it to one of your servants."

But then a temporizing note: "However, for your father David's sake, I will not do this during your lifetime."

Whatever happened to Yahweh's insistence on obedience of the Ten Commandments, "Thou shalt have no other gods before me" and "Thou shalt not commit adultery," to name but two?

BEYOND THIS, IT IS interesting to note how Yahweh trims his sails to the prevailing winds. Solomon's many marriages to foreign women were essentially political and were beneficial to Israel. The shrines to Solomon wives' gods were built not simply for worship but for the convenience of foreign traders in town to do business.

Contrast this with Yahweh's treatment of the outsider, Jephthah. Yahweh uses Jephthah to achieve his purpose – defeating the Ammonites – and that accomplished, callously requires Jephthah to keep his vow and sacrifice his only daughter.

In the Bible women are secondary creatures and relatively unimportant. Jephthah's daughter's life can be snuffed out because of what her father (not she) did, and it is of no moment to Yahweh. Solomon may acquire many wives and engage (presumably, although one gasps at the thought!) in some three hundred extramarital sexual relationships with concubines, but every Israelite woman must come to the marriage bed a virgin and remain faithful to her husband through life or face being stoned to death.

And God is no respecter of persons?

Women were associated with evil and weakness. Indeed, Israelite males sometimes thanked God in the synagogue that they had not been born women. Jesus, conversely, associated freely with women and evidently enjoyed their company, as they did his. The record says that Mary Magdalene and other women provided funds for Jesus and the apostles "out of their means." He demonstrated a concern for the plight of women in the male-dominated society, and this may well have been the reason for his flat-out refusal to sanction divorce on any grounds – under Mosaic law the woman was legally much more vulnerable than the man.

The New Testament frequently reveals Jesus' concern for women. Once when he was a guest in a Pharisee's home, a woman, described by Luke as a sinner (presumably a prostitute), wet Jesus' feet with her tears, dried them with the hair of her head, anointed them with an expensive oil, and repeatedly kissed them. Simon, the Pharisee, concluding that Jesus could not be a prophet or he would have recognized that the woman was a whore, voiced his disapproval. Jesus rebuked him for his judgemental attitude and then said to the woman, "Your sins are forgiven. Go in peace."

There were no women in Jesus' band of apostles, but there would have been compelling reasons for this. Jesus and the disciples travelled frequently, often daily, invariably on foot. Often they slept out in the open. In the circumstances it would have been impossible – and potentially scandalous – for a woman to be a part of that male group.

Despite occasional exceptions, the woman's subsidiary role enforced in the Old Testament was continued in the New.

To judge by his epistles, the apostle Paul was a confirmed misogynist. Writing as mentor to Timothy at Ephesus and giving him instructions to be passed on to the Christian assembly there, he laid down these injunctions:

> I direct the women to wear suitable clothes and to dress quietly and modestly; not with braided hair, gold, jewellery, or expensive clothes. Their adornment is to be the doing of good deeds of the kind that are proper for women who profess religion. During instruction women are to remain silent and submissive. I permit no woman to teach or to tell a man what to do.

His reason? "Because Adam was formed first, then Eve. Bear in mind, it was not Adam who was led astray and fell into sin, but the woman." Paul does concede, however, that "a woman may be saved through bearing children; provided, that is, that she remains modest and is constant in faith, love, and holiness."

Paul again:

> Wives should regard their husbands as they regard the Lord, since, just as Christ is head of the church so the husband is head of his wife. And just as the church submits to Christ, so

should wives submit to their husbands in everything. The husband is the head of the wife as Christ is the head of the church.

In his first letter to the church at Corinth, Paul states unequivocally that men and women have a different status before God. A man, for instance, need not cover his head in the synagogue: "For man is the image and glory of God, but woman is the glory of man – for man was not made from woman but woman from man."

In the same epistle he goes on to say: "Women should keep silent in the churches. They are not permitted to speak. As the Law says, 'They are to be subordinate.' If there is anything a woman wants to know, she should ask her husband after they get home. It is shameful for a woman to speak in church."

Most Protestant churches (even those that hold that the scriptures are the inerrant Word of God) deliberately ignore – as well they might! – these instructions. After many centuries, during which these edicts were more or less obeyed, most churches have bowed to the changing times. There is an increasing number of women clergy and a host of women teachers, although, compared to men, the number remains small. But even this baby step forward took the better part of two thousand years to achieve, and most of these changes were not widely accepted until this century.

The Roman church remains today a male preserve. Women may counsel and assist but, with few exceptions, they may not lead. They may be more numerous than men in the pews and more active in doing good works, but in the majority of the basic expressions of Christianity, women remain subject to and secondary to men.

However, there has been a significant change in the Roman Catholic church in recent years in its attitude to Mary, the mother of Jesus. She is undoubtedly the most celebrated, the most venerated, and the most prayed to of all the saints, being recognized not only as the "Mother of God" but also as "Queen of the Universe." There has been a move among Catholics in recent years to upgrade Mary's eminence even further, possibly to elevate her to a status that could lead to her being regarded as a member of the Godhead. Much of this increased veneration of Mary has come at the instigation of the present Pope, John Paul II, who apparently believes that it was her personal intercession that saved his life during the assassination attempt in St. Peter's Square, Rome, in 1981.

All this despite the fact that Mary played only a minor role in Jesus' adult life and ministry. There are but three references to her after his childhood. The first is at the beginning of his ministry, during the wedding in Cana of Galilee, where he appears to speak to her rudely. The second is when she comes to a house in which he is teaching. Someone tells him, "Your mother and your brothers are here." On the cross, his mother is mentioned as one of three women "standing afar off." And he is said to entrust her to the care of someone thought to be the apostle John.

The Christian church has often claimed to be the champion of women, the compassionate defender of widows and orphans. And sometimes it has been. But through most of history and into the twentieth century women have had to battle tenaciously even to begin to approach actual equality with men. More often than not, even these goals have been achieved despite rather than because of the leadership of the church.

Women in the Church

*T*hroughout the history of humankind women have played a secondary role in virtually every society. The reason for this male dominance is as obvious as the man's larger size and musculature. There have been exceptions but they have been just that, exceptions. In Greek mythology, the Amazons were a tribe of warlike women who established a matriarchal society in Asia Minor in which women governed and waged war and men performed the household tasks.

Alas, ladies! – 'tis but a myth.

This ages-old dominance by men has, however, diminished dramatically in the twentieth century, particularly in the Western world where women have reached the point where there are few positions of authority to which they cannot aspire. Women have become political leaders, presidents of great universities, major players in the worlds of business, finance, medicine, science, and the arts – in virtually every area where size and strength are not a prerequisite.

The one area where this has not been so is in organized religion. Jewish women in Orthodox synagogues – as has been true since time immemorial – may not sit with or participate with the men and are required to remain silent (this is not so in Conservative or Reform synagogues). Christian women, too, have been marginalized over the centuries and it is only in recent decades that they have begun to be recognized as equals and admitted to positions of leadership.

As we have seen, the one church in which women have made the least progress is the largest and the oldest – the Roman Catholic church. The present Pope, John Paul II – despite the conflicting views of a majority of the church's women members and not a few of the clergy – remains adamantly opposed to premarital sex, the use of contraceptive devices, legal abortion, and the consecration of women as priests.

As recently as 1965, Pope Paul VI in the encyclical *Humanae Vitae* (Of Human Life) reaffirmed the papal principle that every act of sexual intercourse "must be open to the transmission of life." Despite this, the evidence is clear that a large majority of married couples, including many married theologians, do not agree. They argue, in increasing numbers, that contraception, by some means, is a moral and pragmatic necessity in a marriage where the partners love each other and need to express that love physically while, at the same time, controlling the size of their family.

Increasingly, the Roman Catholic laity is making clear its opposition to the rigidity of their church in matters related to sex. As noted earlier, a recent sampling in Canada by the Angus Reid polling organization indicated that 91 per cent of Catholics approve the use of contraceptives. Moreover, 84 per cent would permit priests to marry and 78 per cent believe that women should be to allowed to become priests.

This change in attitude is increasingly evident in every branch of the Christian church – Catholic, Protestant, and what have you. Women are insisting that they play a larger and more significant role. And they are being heard. Women now teach in Catholic seminaries, direct diocesan chanceries and, in some parishes, fulfil virtually all of a priest's responsibilities but the most important ones – saying Mass and hearing confessions. And the pressure for change is increasing apace. A growing number of Catholics, men and women, are speaking out for the democratic election of priests and for optional celibacy – some are even contending for the blessing of the church on the marriages of gay men and women.

"The times they are a-changin'."

In November 1992, the Church of England, after a passionate debate, decided (by a margin of only three votes) to nullify the rule that only men may serve as priests. By approving the ordination of women, some thirteen hundred women deacons were made eligible for the priesthood. It should be added that, shortly afterward, a large number of adamantly opposed priests announced that they planned to leave the church and would consider joining the Roman church, from which the Church of England separated in 1534 over the Pope's refusal to grant Henry VIII an annulment of his marriage to Catharine of Aragon.

Hardly a ringing endorsement of women's rights!

In voting for the ordination of women priests, the Church of England was following the lead of its sister Anglican churches in Canada, Australia, and New Zealand. They were preceded by many other church bodies in various parts of the world. Some of these:

- 1948: the African Methodist Episcopal Church approved the ordination of women.
- 1956: the Methodist and Presbyterian churches in the United States voted to allow women clergy.
- 1958: the Lutheran Church in Sweden agreed to ordain women.
- 1970: the Lutheran Church in the U.S.A. voted to do the same.
- 1975: the Anglican Church of Canada approved women priests.
- 1976: the Episcopal Church in the U.S.A. approved women priests.
- 1980: the first woman bishop in the Methodist Church, U.S.A.
- 1989: the first woman bishop in the Episcopal Church, U.S.A.
- 1992: the first woman bishop in the Lutheran Church, Germany.
- 1992: the first woman bishop in the Lutheran Church, U.S.A.

In the face of all this change the Roman Catholic hierarchy remains inflexible. To be a priest in the Roman church you must be a man. Nor may a woman be installed as a bishop, an archbishop, a cardinal, or pope. Nor may a woman hear confessions or officiate at the Mass. A woman may be consecrated to serve as a "sister," but she may not aspire to or be appointed to any position of sacramental authority.

Evil and Good

God – and Evil

*I*s there anyone who has not asked some of the following questions?

- If there is an omnipotent and loving God, why does he permit earthquakes, hurricanes, droughts, and other natural disasters to kill indiscriminately tens of thousands of men, women, and children?
- How could a loving God originate as part of his creation such horrible illnesses as encephalitis, cerebral palsy, the various cancers, leprosy, Alzheimer's, and other incurable diseases, and permit them indiscriminately to afflict tens of thousands of men, women, and children?
- When an earthquake in Turkey buries thousands alive, when a typhoon drowns 150,000 Pakistanis over a weekend, when a drought in Somalia kills thousands of men, women, and children by starvation, why does a loving God not do *something* to help the helpless?
- How could a loving God create an endless hell and consign the majority of the world's people to it, year after year, century after century, simply because they do not worship him?

WHAT HAS BEEN CALLED "the problem of evil" has puzzled men and women of every generation in every part of the world. Why, in a world created by a loving and omnipotent God, are disease, suffering, and death an inescapable part of life? What is the reason for it? The theologians have attempted to address the question and have offered a variety of answers, but none of them are convincing.

Most of the horrors cannot simply be attributed to or blamed on humankind's sinfulness – so many of those who hunger and suffer and die are decent men, women, and children. Some are babes in arms. When an earthquake or a plague devastates an area, killing thousands and leaving tens of thousands injured and other thousands homeless, or when a prolonged drought turns productive soil into a desert, the people stricken by these natural disasters are not the wicked getting what they deserve; they are more often than not the poor, the defenceless, and the children.

We have come to understand something about natural disasters and are sometimes able to ameliorate their impact, but we are not the cause of them and can do little if anything to control them. A meteorologist may accurately predict the onset of a hurricane, a geologist may warn of an imminent earthquake, but neither can keep them from happening. They are, quite simply, beyond human control.

The insurance companies continue to call them acts of God.

THERE IS ALSO A host of personal disasters over which we have little or no control. They include incapacitating illnesses, genetic defects, metabolic disorders, and those physiological or psychological aberrations that produce such horrors as Down's syndrome in the newborn and Alzheimer's in the aging. The victims and those who love them often suffer piteously. A foetus may be hopelessly afflicted before it is born. Some have been called "human vegetables." Others cannot breathe without a respirator. Many of the aged are afflicted with brain or motor degeneration. Flesh and bone diminish, the body wasting away to the point where the individual is as much as dead.

Indeed, in some cases they would be better off dead.

BUT THERE ARE OTHER kinds of suffering, many that have nothing to do with natural disasters or with disease. A member of the congregation of which I was the minister, a zestful, intelligent, and beautiful woman in her early twenties, was so afflicted. I officiated at her wedding. The man she married was personable, intelligent, and apparently successful in business, but he proved to be an inveterate liar and physically abusive. And he deserted her a few months into the marriage when he learned she was pregnant – emptying their joint bank account as he left.

The pregnancy palliated her sorrow somewhat. The life growing within her gave her hope and purpose and a reason to live.

I visited her in hospital the day her child was born. She was heavily sedated, and when roused by the nurse looked at me through vacant eyes. When I held her hand and spoke to her, she made no response. The baby, I was informed by the nurse, had been born hydrocephalic and would die within days. I was shown the infant: a boy, quivering spasmodically in a respirator, the upper part of his head twice normal size and visibly pulsing with the heartbeat.

Later that week I performed the child's funeral. It was private. I can't recall what I said – I'm sure it was all the obligatory things: vapid statements about how God's ways are not ours and are often mysterious and beyond human understanding; but that we must have faith in his divine purpose, believing that, one day, it will all become clear . . .

Afterwards, I said nothing. I simply held the woman in my arms, trying to will strength into her while she wept great, shuddering sobs. I hadn't the wisdom – or the temerity – to offer the usual explanations.

Her tragedy was soul-destroying. But consider for a moment the millions of children in the Third World who are cursed from the day they are born: by their sickly bodies, their indifferent parents, and their place of birth. They grow up in slums, in many instances lacking home and family and affection. They suffer from those deficiencies and illnesses caused by malnutrition and the poor health of the mother. They are raised in poverty, clothed in rags, illiterate for want of schooling, and from early childhood, forced by events to scratch out a living any way they can.

Millions of children – yes, *millions* – are doomed from the day they are born.

SOME YEARS AGO A missionary friend told me of a girl who came into the world in Calcutta. From her birth and throughout her lifetime she never knew one moment of affection. She was born onto a filthy piece of cardboard in a filthy inner-city dump. Her mother was a teenage prostitute. She suffered from rickets from birth, and as a child of four was put onto the streets to beg. From the age of ten, the man who had fathered her sold her daily to various men for a few rupees. She was dead at the age of fourteen from pneumonia complicated by syphilis and malnutrition.

Hearing about her I was reminded of the little song we sang in Sunday school,

> Jesus loves the little children,
> All the children of the world.
> Black and yellow, red and white,
> They are precious in his sight . . .

CARE International reports that some five million children die each year from cholera simply because they lack clean water to drink. The World Health Organization estimates that forty thousand people a day die from preventable diseases. Thousands of others die in famines such as those in Eritrea, the Sudan, Somalia, and elsewhere. Who can ever erase from their memory the pictures on television showing these men, women and, most pathetically, children – human beings literally starving to death. Mothers with babies, whose limbs are like bundles of dry sticks, held to a dry breast. Children without the energy to cry or raise a hand to drive the flies from their eyes and the corners of their mouths.

Yes, the politicians and the feuding armies and the various warlords in the region are partly to blame – often they appropriate for their own use the shipments of food and medicine sent to the area by foreign governments or charitable institutions – but these children did not choose to be born into this world nor were they or their parents the cause of the drought.

It is sometimes argued that these innocents suffer not so much from nature's failure as from man's inhumanity to man. But surely both are true. Yes, many of them die because evil men do evil, but beyond that and apart from it *they die because there has been no rain!* – something over which neither they nor their parents nor the politicians nor anyone else has any control.

And all the while, other people in other parts of the world are dying by the tens of thousands because there is too *much* rain!

When, in 1989, Hurricane Hugo swept through the Caribbean, it killed hundreds of Jamaicans and left thousands homeless. Every year there are reports from various parts of the world of towns and settlements wiped out by high winds or by what are called "storm surges" – masses of water driven before an oncoming hurricane. Who can forget the reports of the onslaught of the elements that swept across Bangladesh in the spring of 1991, killing 125,000 men, women, and children and leaving ten million homeless.

It was not the first time it had happened.

Nor will it be the last.

Who was not moved to pity in December 1988 by the newspaper and television reports of those Armenian refugees who, driven from their homeland by their traditional enemies, the Turks, fled to the apparent safety of Azerbaijan only to have a violent earthquake kill fifty thousand of them?

THE PERVASIVENESS OF pain and suffering and death is equally horrific in the animal world. It is a world pervaded by – *based on* – suffering and death.

According to the first chapter of Genesis, before God made man he created animals: the great and lesser beasts, the birds, the reptiles, the fish, and "all manner of creeping things." They are all in different degrees sensate creatures. They manifest fear, they feel pain, they suffer and die. Their life and death is part of what has been called nature's grand design.

This being so, one is bound to ask why the loving God found it necessary to base the sustaining of the life of so many of his creatures on killing and devouring? Surely it would not be beyond the competence of an omniscient deity to create an animal world that could be sustained and perpetuated without suffering and death.

Why does God's grand design require creatures with teeth designed to crush spines or rend flesh, claws fashioned to seize and tear, venom to paralyze, mouths to suck blood, coils to constrict and smother – even expandable jaws so that prey may be swallowed whole and alive?

There are three basic types of animal: the herbivorous, the carnivorous, and the omnivorous. The herbivorous ingest plant life, the carnivorous subsist mostly on flesh, and the omnivorous – which includes us – on anything that has nutritive value and can be ingested.

As a consequence:

On land: the big cats kill zebras or wildebeest or impala or any creature they can bring down. Hyenas and jackals kill anything they can overwhelm by numbers. Crocodiles kill anything driven to their waterhole by thirst. Wolves kill hares. Grizzly bears kill salmon. Foxes kill birds and burrowers. So do snakes, which also kill larger prey through the injection of venom or by squeezing the life out of them or by swallowing them alive.

In the waters: whales kill krill, killer whales kill seals, sharks kill porpoises, porpoises kill mullet, sea-lions kill penguins, conger eels kill squid, bass kill fingerlings, mullet kill minnows.

From the air: eagles kill salmon, hawks kill rodents, vultures eat carrion, gulls eat anything they can ingest, alive or dead. On and on, day and night, the maiming, killing, and devouring continues, with all the omnivorous or predatory creatures "doing what comes naturally."

The grim and inescapable reality is that *all life is predicated on death*. Every carnivorous creature *must* kill and devour another creature. It has no option. Meanwhile, all the herbivorous creatures engorge themselves on grasses and grains and berries so that – albeit unwittingly – they may provide nutrition for the carnivores through what is called the food chain.

This is the way the world works. All life is predicated on death. Ingest some living thing or die of starvation.

The reader of these lines – unless he or she is a vegetarian – is alive because a steer or lamb or pig or calf or chicken was butchered and brought to market. In one large Canadian city 12,500 cattle, 8,000 pigs, 2,700 sheep and 50,000 chickens are slaughtered *every day* so that we omnivorous humans may live.

Nor is mercy admitted to the occasion. When animals kill, as often as not the victim's death is painful and protracted. When a pack of hyenas or wild dogs runs down a zebra they first cut it from the herd and then bring it down through sheer numbers. No individual could accomplish the kill. The prey is seized by the muzzle. Another member of the pack clamps onto the tail or fastens on a haunch, and the remainder swarm in to bring the victim to the ground. Hyenas cannot do as a lion might, break the neck or close off the windpipe, and as a consequence their victims die slowly. Usually, because it is the area of easiest access, predators go in through the belly, often beginning to devour the innards while the victim is still alive.

The predators – at whatever level and whatever their method of killing – are not evil; they are doing what they were born to do. *It is the way the world works*, and has been across millions of years as various species of mammals, birds, fish, snakes, and insects – and even humans – have perpetuated themselves by eating one another.

Nature is, in Tennyson's vivid phrase, "red in tooth and claw," and life is a carnival of blood.

The grand design also includes the creation of parasites: worms, fleas, ticks, lice are themselves unable to kill, but following their destiny, are capable of penetrating the skin, burrowing into the body, or flourishing in the lungs, bloodstream, or digestive system, often destroying the health of and sometimes killing the host creature, and generally making life miserable.

On an even more minuscule scale are the bacteria, the viruses, the aberrant cells that attack the body or the organs or the brain, and the malignant cells that stimulate abnormal growth or the development of diseased tissue.

CONSIDER FOR A MOMENT the epidemics or plagues that in every age have devastated the population in various parts of the world. The word plague is used to describe any contagious, malignant, epidemic disease. The bubonic plague and the black plague – so named because multiple haemorrhages beneath the skin turned it black – were two forms of the same disease, one transmitted by fleas from infected rats, the other by infected squirrels, rabbits, and chipmunks. The afflicted died in three to four days. And there was no cure.

The earliest visitation of which there is a record took place in Europe in 430 B.C. and began in Athens. An outbreak in Rome in the third century B.C. killed as many as five thousand men, women, and children *daily*.

The most widespread plague in Western history began in Constantinople in 1334 and moved through Europe – spread in part by the returning Crusaders who had been off killing infidels to the greater glory of God. It is estimated by historians that, in fewer than twenty years, that particular plague killed as much as three-quarters of the population of Europe and Asia. In untreated cases – and there was little if any treatment available – the mortality rate ran as high as 90 per cent.

After Columbus "discovered" the Americas he was followed there by the Spanish conquistadores, who brought with them various European diseases. The Latin American Indians had no antibodies to protect them and sickened and died in uncounted numbers. In Brazil alone, the pre-conquest population of 2.4 million was reduced to slightly more than 200,000.

Today, we are facing a relatively new international plague – AIDS. The cause is the HIV virus. There is no known cure. The virus spreads by passing directly from the blood of an infected person into the blood of an uninfected person – or, less commonly, through semen or saliva. In North America it is primarily (although not exclusively) a homosexual disease, but in parts of Africa, where the disease is rampant, it most commonly afflicts heterosexuals, men, women, and their children alike.

Let me add to this list of physical afflictions that degeneration of the human brain commonly called Alzheimer's disease.

Alzheimer's is a geriatric illness that diminishes and even erases memory, and in its late stages obliterates any sense of personal identity and family relationships. The Alzheimer's sufferer may manifest few physical symptoms, may not be confined to bed, and may be able to function in many ways, but – and this is surely the ultimate loss – *he no longer knows who he is!*

In its later stages, the victim of the disease cannot be permitted to leave his place of residence alone because he cannot recall where he lives, those he lives with, or even his own name, and within a city block from home can become hopelessly lost.

How by any reach of the imagination can this bizarre and tragic affliction serve any good end? It commonly destroys marriages, parenthood, friendships, and a sense of family – the things on which most loving relationships are predicated – and replaces them with quarrelsomeness, rancour, resentment, estrangement, despair, and finally, death.

How, one must ask, could a loving Heavenly Father so order it? Alzheimer's is not a punishment for wrongdoing; it does not afflict only the wicked. It seems to be genetically destined and strikes indiscriminately and without apparent cause both the decent and the reprobate. Perhaps the worst aspect of the illness is that it destroys not only the victim but the victim's loved ones. For the families of Alzheimer's sufferers, it is as though the loved one had died and been resurrected as an irascible look-alike stranger. Love and affection has been replaced by estrangement, suspicion, and resentment. Somewhere in the brain of the individual the past has been erased.

HOW COULD A LOVING and omnipotent God create such horrors as we have been contemplating? Jesus said: "Are not five sparrows sold for a penny, and not one of them is forgotten before God; and are you not of more value than many sparrows?" But if God grieves over the death of one sparrow, how could even his eternal spirit bear the sickness, suffering, and death of the multiplied millions of men, women, children, animals, birds, and other sensate creatures, in every part of the world, in every century since time began?

Especially when he would know that it all stems from his creativity!

The inescapable answer is that "a loving God" could not possibly be the author of the horrors we have been describing – horrors that continue every day, have continued since time began, and will continue as long as life exists. It is an inconceivable tale of suffering and death, and because the tale is fact – is, in truth, the history of the world – it is obvious that there cannot be a loving God.

Good – and Evil

The Christian church teaches a dichotomy of good and evil: God and Satan, Heaven and Hell, saints and sinners, angels and devils, the saved and the lost.

Natural phenomena such as sunshine and the gentle rain are part of the good and are said to be gifts from God. Misfortunes such as natural catastrophes, disease, and death are taken to be the work of a malign spirit, the Devil.

These are, of course, primitive and simplistic views of life. Some so-called "evil" forces achieve good. A hurricane howling through a forest may bring mature trees crashing to the ground, but their destruction enables the sun to penetrate to the forest floor, stimulating new growth.

The Hawaiian islands are perhaps the most beautiful area on earth but they were born of unimaginable volcanic violence on the ocean floor. Much of the islands' unique beauty derives from the fertility of the soil, but this fertility is, in large part, a result of the decomposition of volcanic materials rich in minerals. Even the ash produces revenue for the islanders: it is an excellent cleaning and polishing agent and is sold around the world.

IN THE EARLY beginnings of society attempts were made to explain the existence of good and evil by attributing them to the gods or other supernatural beings. Having no explanation for the various manifestations of nature, men assumed that they were the work of benign or malign spirits and specific acts of worship were developed to curry favour with the beneficent spirits or to placate the evil ones.

The histories of most of the peoples of earth include legends about the origin of the world and themselves and these became the grounds of their religion. Some of the legends posit gods or pantheons of gods, good or demonic spirits. Some personalize the beneficent sun and the sometimes baleful moon. The elements, the seasons, the natural forces were deified, as were birds and animals: the imperious lion, the soaring eagle, the wily serpent, the Leviathan in the seas . . .

Most of these legends incorporate myths about the origins of good and evil. In some there is a three-tiered world: a paradise, a world of everyday life, and a nether world, and, controlling these, gods and demons. A number include bizarre explanations for the origins of men and women and the higher animals. Some stipulate rewards from the gods for certain actions and punishment or banishment for others. Some envision life beyond the grave as a series of incarnations in which there are opportunities to better one's state.

Many Christians assume that the Genesis story of the creation of the heavens and the earth is unique, but other religions and other peoples have their own legends: among them the Islamics, the Celts, the Chinese, the Egyptians, the Greeks, the Romans, the Japanese, the Scandinavians, the Slavonics, the Tibetans, the Zoroastrians.

It is a Judeo-Christian conceit that the Great Flood of Noah's time is historic fact and is unique, but there are flood myths in the legends of American and Australian aboriginals and in the traditions of the Chinese, Greek, Hindu, Melanesian, Mesopotamian and Mithraic peoples.

As places of punishment for wrongdoing, there are a host of "hells." Some exist to purify and prepare the individual for entry into another life. Others offer paths to higher levels of being. In some – including the Christian myth – both the bliss of Heaven and the horrors of Hell are without end.

ROBUST HEALTH, MENTAL acuity, and a sense of *joie de vivre* make life on earth something to celebrate. But there is another side to the coin

– disease, suffering, and death can turn life's joys into ashes. Just as a Jesus of Nazareth may issue from a virgin's womb in Palestine, a Muhammad come to birth in Mecca, and a Mahatma Gandhi enter into life in India, and each leave behind ineradicable legacies, another woman's pregnancy may terminate with the birth of a brain-damaged or crippled infant and lead to a lifetime of sadness and despair.

The game of life is played with a loaded deck. It deals – often for no apparent reason – hearts or diamonds to some and spades or clubs to others. Some enter the world with the proverbial silver spoon in the mouth, others are born to trouble. The phrase "life is hell" is an appropriate description of the lot of millions of men, women, and children in the Third World. There is no measuring or imagining the horrors they endure. Tens of thousands live daily with pain and without hope. As has been said of them: "They are the people God forgot."

But to focus only on the tragedy and suffering in the world is to distort reality. There is so much in life that is good: the beauty and bounty of the earth; the bonding of a man and a woman; the joy in a long-delayed reunion with loved ones; the contemplation of great music and great art; the sense of completion when a woman is handed her newborn; the pleasure in the company of friends; the satisfaction of a long-sought goal achieved; loving and being loved. There is the unspeakable horror of the Nazi Holocaust, but there is also the soaring beauty of a Mozart symphony, a Michelangelo painting, a Pavlova's grace, one of those "perfect" days in June . . .

"Good" and "evil." They are each, inevitably, inescapably part of the way life is.

WE HUMANS ARE UNIQUE among living creatures. We are the only members of the "animal kingdom" with a highly developed capacity for sequential and abstract thought. We alone have the ability to examine complex data and reach a logical conclusion. But there is the other side of the coin: because of this unique gift we alone are capable of *choosing* to do evil. This is the reason societies find it necessary to establish laws and inflict punishments designed specifically to deter antisocial behaviour.

We have created police forces and built prisons to protect ourselves from ourselves. Nations have found it necessary to arm their
borders and to take joint action to restrain aggressor nations and have
sometimes had to intervene with force of arms through instruments
such as the United Nations. There has never been a moment in history
since records began that does not list wars, invasions, insurrections,
betrayals, torture, atrocities, and other similar examples of man's
inhumanity to man.

FOR ALL OUR VAUNTED progress, with the skyrocketing increase
in information and ability in the twentieth century, has our world
become a better place?

Undoubtedly, yes. Better – and worse. We are better for widespread literacy, for "miracle" medications and modern hospitals, for
the ability to turn night into day with the touch of a switch. We can
keep ourselves warm in winter and cool in summer, drink pure water
by turning a spigot, preserve our abundance so that it is available in
times of scarcity, quest for the wisdom of the past and the present in
films and public libraries, capture entertainment in a box, record our
thoughts without a pen, transmit them around the world in seconds,
and store them permanently with the touch of a button. We can move
about at will on land or sea, in the air, and beneath the waters, con-
verse from our homes or offices with friends or family or business
associates around the world, watch distant events even as they happen, even live in outer space. Today's world is truly One World in the
sense that no place is distant from any other.

We live in a time of unmatched progress. There have been more
improvements in our way of living in the past one hundred years than
in the previous two thousand. It is undoubtedly a more advanced and
comfortable world than at any time in history, but is it a better world?
The names Belsen, Buchenwald, Auschwitz, Rwanda, Iraq, Bosnia,
the Soviet Union, North Korea make it evident that it is not. Add to
this list natural disasters – earthquakes, floods, hurricanes, droughts
– and such new terrors as AIDS, the easy availability of narcotic drugs,
and increasing juvenile crime and we are reminded that evil is always
with us, in abundance.

Listen to the international news on any given night and some report will leave even the eternal optimist less than sanguine.

HOW HAVE WE REACTED to the improvements in technology, convenience, and communication?

- By fighting the bloodiest wars in history.
- By developing a record number of neuroses and psychosomatic illnesses.
- By increasing exponentially juvenile crime.
- By proliferating the ownership of guns and assault-weapons.
- By developing a means of destruction that can obliterate an entire city and every living creature in it.

Professor Pitirim Sorokin of Harvard University, after a study of the more than nine hundred international and civil wars in the past fifty years, came to the conclusion that "our century is, by far, the bloodiest in history."

Aldous Huxley, the British philosopher, said: "Our technological progress now makes it possible to move *backward* more rapidly."

We have made astonishing advances in many fields, but we seem to acquire knowledge without acquiring wisdom. We know more than any people in history. Any modern library is an intellectual bank in which the giants of the past have made deposit and on which we may draw at no cost other than the expenditure of time. Such has been the increase in the stock of information that ours has become, of necessity, an age of specialists – no one person can assimilate all the available information in any given field.

Most of us live better than any people in history. The modern house is a marvel of convenience and comfort and makes one wonder how, a generation ago, the mother of a large family got her work done. Before the days of electricity, refrigerators, dishwashers, vacuum cleaners, electric kitchen utensils, supermarkets, frozen foods, preservatives, and packaged food, how *did* she get her work done?

The answer is, of course, she didn't. And as a consequence, her life expectancy was diminished.

But coincident with the dramatic improvements in our modern cities has come a comparable increase in violent crime and the continual lowering of the average age of our criminals, and this has made the centre of many of our great cities – with their proliferation of guns, muggings, gang wars, and drive-by shootings – the civic equivalent of a war zone. In some of the wealthiest, most technologically advanced cities in the history of civilization, no outsider can walk the downtown streets at midnight without the likelihood of being robbed, mugged, and perhaps killed.

ON THE DAY OF THE Pentecost the apostle Peter stood before a crowd in Jerusalem and cried out, "Save yourself from this untoward generation." Any schoolchild will understand all the words in the sentence except one – what is an *untoward* generation? In contemporary times a host of Peters are saying, "Save yourself from this violent, unruly, intractable, aimless, out-of-control generation, with everyone forever on the go but few getting anywhere."

For many, life is a crazy quilt made up of snippets and patches and lacking design; it has become a rat race, with no goal and no purpose. If, at the turn of this century, a man missed his train, he might shrug his shoulders and say, "Oh, that's all right; there'll be another one tomorrow." Today, if we go downtown and miss the first section of a revolving door we feel behind schedule for the rest of the day.

The reader may interject: "Okay. But what has this to do with evil?" The answer is this: life is precious – the most precious commodity in the universe – and if it is trivialized or disdained it is the ultimate waste.

The Way the World Works

*D*espite the fact that many in the Christian church teach it and millions of Christians believe it, humankind did not come into being a few thousand years ago in an Edenic garden but millions of years ago when a tree-dwelling hominid decided that it would be advantageous to forage on the African savannah. We today are one result of that decision.

In the dim mists of prehistory early man acquired the skills necessary for the development and perpetuity of human life. Among them were these basics:

- Self-perpetuation: the need to reproduce and nurture.
- Co-operation: the willingness to work with others.
- Comprehension: the ability to learn from experience.

Without offspring the early hominids would have disappeared from the earth in a generation. Without a willingness to join hands in a common task, they would have been limited in what they could do. And without the development of the brain, they would have – as thousands of their contemporaries did – ended as fossilized artifacts. These basic laws remain true in our time: no individual, no family, no nation can persevere and prosper unless it reproduces, co-operates with others, and learns from experience.

Co-operation is fundamental to the survival of any society. When, during the dim beginnings of human existence, a landslide or the fall of a great tree blocked an essential trail in the forest, only a co-ordinated effort could remove it. Attacks by roving marauders could only be repulsed if individuals banded together. And when it became essential to track down prey or dam a river or build a palisade or a common house, planning and co-operation were essential.

Civilization emerged and developed because men and women came to realize that "no man is an island" and that they could not exist, much less flourish, without one another.

Early man learned also that there are laws intrinsic to life and that they must be obeyed. Obey them and personal survival and community living is possible; break them and they will break you.

It is the way the world works and it has nothing to do with a deity.

We give names to these natural laws; the law of gravity is one. Gravity is the attracting force existing between particles of matter. Any matter, whether a single atom or a body as large as our sun, exists in a relationship to all other matter. Every body in the universe is attracted to every other body by a force that is stronger the more massive the body and the closer its proximity to another body.

And it is this law of gravity, this natural law, that makes existence possible. Without it our bodies would not have evolved as they have. Today, because of the adaptation of our bones and muscles to the pull of gravity, controlled upright movement is possible. If gravity were a random or erratic rather than an intrinsic force, our evolution as human beings *could* not have happened.

THERE ARE MANY natural laws, most of them less important than the law of gravity but all of them fundamental to the perpetuation of life. Among them, as an example, are laws that relate to the maintenance of one's physical well-being. One of these is, "Thou shalt not be a glutton." Why not? Because gluttony eventually kills you. Eat sensibly – no other factors impinging – and you will live. Don't, and you won't. It's "the law" and it has nothing to do with one's faith or lack of faith or with the pleasure or displeasure of a god.

It is, quite simply, the way the world works.

LET ME POSIT another example: The Pope is seriously ill. A devout Roman Catholic sister vows to undertake a prayer vigil and fast until God grants her prayer to save the life of the Pope. Days pass, then weeks. The pontiff remains in a coma, kept alive by the skills of his doctors and the resources of modern medicine. The sister becomes emaciated and dies. The following week the Pope dies. They both died as a result of the operation of natural law but it had nothing to do with God.

It is the way the world works.

A further example: The bestial and corrupt dictator of a Middle Eastern country orders an attack on a neighbouring nation. He is a vain man who prides himself on his fitness, working out daily and controlling his diet. The invasion is a success but thousands die on the field of battle. The dictator is solely responsible for the carnage but there is no divine punishment for his actions. He lives out his life in luxury and dies peacefully in his sleep at the age of ninety.

Laws related to the maintenance of the body's health killed the Pope and the Catholic sister. The observance of those laws helped preserve the corrupt politician. Nature's laws are impersonal and have nothing to do with justice or with an individual's faith in God.

Again, we never do break the laws fundamental to life; we break ourselves *on* the laws.

WE HAVE BEEN EXAMINING the effects of various physical laws on humans, but there are other laws, intangible, not subject to examination under a microscope or in isolation in a test tube but just as real in their effects. Among these are the laws that function in human relationships. Love and you will be loved. Hate and you will be hated. Be friendly and you will have friends. Lie and deceive and no one will believe you when you tell the truth. Act violently and others will respond violently. Pat a dog and it will lick your hand; kick it and it will bite you.

It's the law.

These universal "laws" require no carved stone tablets or angelic messenger to reveal them, no divine commands from heaven to activate them; they are, quite simply the way the world works.

From the beginning of time and in every part of the world, emerging human societies have found it expedient to establish rules of behaviour with appropriate penalties for disobedience. Invariably, a group of men – priests, politicians, shamans, holy men, witch doctors, or what have you – codify these rules, proclaim them as eternal truth, and insist that a deity requires obedience to them. These edicts thus become divine commandments. Penalties for disobedience – even for disbelief – are established. Punishments are inflicted for infractions and the clergy warn of retribution even beyond the grave. Rulers find these laws essential to maintaining order, so obedience is made mandatory and is enforced by punishment in this world and threats of punishment in the next.

For most men and women in the civilized world, life is good most of the time, and many attribute these "blessings" to a loving Heavenly Father. But life has another side, a seamy side, a dark side: disease, suffering, disappointment, despair, and death. It would not, however, be politic to blame the loving God for these, so, early on, the theologians posited an "adversary" – variously known as Satan, the Devil, Beelzebub, the Evil One – and laid the blame for life's heartbreaks and sorrows on him.

But surely it is time to recognize that the good and the bad, the blessings and the heartbreaks are not acts of God or works of the Devil, they are no more and no less than manifestations of natural law.

PERHAPS THIS CAN best be seen by examining the functioning of the natural world and noting that nothing in it is intrinsically good or evil. It simply *is*. Consider the enormous potential for both good and evil in something as uncomplicated as a drop of water.

Observe it, glistening on the tip of your finger. It was born of the combination of two invisible gases. It is two-thirds hydrogen and one-third oxygen and is now visible – a tiny drop of crystal-clear liquid, the most plentiful substance on earth.

Separate the hydrogen from the oxygen and it becomes a gas. Multiply it and it will inflate a balloon or lift a dirigible. Separate the oxygen from the hydrogen and it will save the life of a man struggling to breathe.

Combine the drop of water with others and you have a gentle spring rain, stirring life in millions of dormant seeds, resuscitating the grasses and grains and flowers and trees, creating beauty for the eye and food for the body and offering the gift of life to every living thing from an amoeba to a human being.

Vaporize many such drops of water and they become a mist, clinging to its mother on a northern lake or reaching up to form a rainbow in the morning sun. On the far horizon the individual drops of water form a great cloud-bank, a mass of vapour limned with gold and, as the day dies, capturing the sun and fashioning it into a display of colour that ravishes the eye.

Transform the drop of water into a single snowflake. Place it under a microscope and it will reveal a geometric complexity that is astonishing in its intricacy. Combine it with other snowflakes – billions of them, no two identical – and they will blanket the earth, contouring the land and issuing an invitation to every child to frolic in its glinting, padded beauty.

On a sultry summer day this drop of water may join with others to form a fresh mountain spring. Cup your hands in the sparkling waters and bring them to your lips. Instant refreshment! Dive into a cool pond and the gentle flow over your body will invigorate your flagging spirits.

Fill a kettle, heat it, and the steam will whistle a happy tune of refreshment in a cup of tea. Fill a plastic tub with warm water, immerse an infant in it, and he will splash and squeal with delight.

But, just as the gentle rain can stimulate nature's bounty and call forth her beauty and variety, it can as easily turn into an instrument of death and destruction. Combine our single drop with millions of others and you have a torrent that can carry away the soil, run foaming and laden in the ditches, tumble in a tossing torrent into a valley, rip up a giant oak by the roots, convert houses into debris and leave hundreds homeless or spreadeagled in untidy death on a heap of debris.

The cool pond may refresh you, but fall into it from a great height and it will break every bone in your body. Multiply our snowflake and it can create great drifts on a mountain peak, gleaming with breathtaking beauty in the morning sun. Later in the day it can come roaring down in an avalanche that can bury a village and destroy every living thing in its path. A single snowflake can fuse with others and, over the months, inch its way to the ocean's edge to break off as an iceberg that can rupture the steel plates of a great ship and take a thousand lives.

Water . . .

Is it good? Is it evil? It is neither. In all its many manifestations it simply *is*. As is true of everything else in our world it is a part of the operation of natural law. It can be a benison or a curse but it *is* neither. It is a part of the way things are, have been for billions of years, and will be in the millennia to come.

It has nothing to do with a god.

Our Impersonal World

*A*lthough there is no deity even remotely like the anthropomorphic God of the Bible, life on earth does not function randomly or by chance. As we have seen, our world is not a chaotic place; it is governed by natural law. Obey these laws and, normally, life is orderly and enjoyable, break them and we discover that we don't in fact break the laws, we break ourselves *on* the laws; the laws remain unchanged.

Our world is not a unique or new phenomenon; it is a minuscule part of an expanding universe, a universe that has existed over billions of years in a continual state of evolutionary change. Nor is it a universe created by or governed by a deity in some hypothetical heaven. Despite its volatility and its sometime apparent randomness, it is subject – as everything that exists is subject – to natural law. And these natural laws are not capricious; it is an orderly universe and its immutable and dependable order is what makes life possible.

Early in prehistory our predecessors learned by experience how to co-operate with the world of which they were a part. They came to understand that since all life is governed by natural laws they must obey these laws or suffer the consequences. They learned that the failure to do could lead to pain or deprivation or death. They learned also that, while it is an orderly universe, it is impersonal, and, to put it bluntly, it doesn't give a damn about you or me, the President, the Prime Minister, the Pope, or anyone else. And we, if we wish to exist in our infinitesimally tiny corner of the universe,

must obey the natural law in its various manifestations or pay the
penalty for our disobedience.

BELIEVING THAT THE world had been created by a "personal"
God, the men who wrote the Bible concluded that when misfortune
befell them – illnesses, droughts, natural disasters, events beyond
their control – they were afflictions imposed by their God, and were
evidence that they had earned his displeasure.

Conversely, when things went well, when one's health was robust,
when harvests were plentiful and enemies were vanquished, it was
taken as evidence that God was pleased with them and on their side.

Other tribes and peoples did the same, and as time passed,
prophets, soothsayers, shamans, medicine-men, astrologers, priests,
clergymen, and their like emerged, each claiming to be privy to the
deity's will. These men – and they were invariably men – worked out
a theology of sorts, asserted that it was requisite to worship and placate the gods in specific ways and that the failure to do so would lead
to punishment, not only in this life but sometimes beyond the grave.

Over the centuries these various self-proclaimed "holy men"
imposed on their particular societies a variety of rules, asserting that
they were God's laws. They were in fact concepts born out of the
shrewd observation of human behaviour plus a keen eye for human
weakness. Inevitably, things went well or ill for every citizen and every
tribe. The good was attributed to God and the bad to the Devil.

NATURAL LAW FUNCTIONS everywhere and in everything. You
can see it in arithmetic where two plus two equals four – not sometimes, not randomly, but every time. Break the laws of arithmetic and
numbers become bereft of meaning, business will be reduced to
barter, and nothing will have a fixed value. The immutability of natural law makes commerce possible.

Because the natural laws are universal and intrinsic, we can use
them in daily life. The consistency of the law of gravity, for example,
makes mobility possible. It enables you to take a step without being
unpredictably rivetted to the spot or rocketed into the sky. We utilize
the laws of aerodynamics to design aircraft that enable us to fly.

Through our understanding of the laws of volatility we control the explosions of gasoline in the cylinder of an engine and thus increase our mobility. We use the laws of displacement to build a great ship and travel the oceans. We use the laws of soil fertility to produce food. We employ the laws of procreation to create other human beings and to breed various animals for use as sources of power, transportation, and food.

"Mother Nature" is a term sometimes used to describe the operation of natural law. And she can be a beneficent mistress. Obey nature's laws and life can yield rich rewards, among them fresh air, pure water, bountiful harvests, fragrant flowers, and dazzling sunsets. But disobey nature's laws and she will punish you with polluted air and water, floods, droughts, crop failures, and famine.

It's the law. It's the way the world works. And it has nothing to do with the actions or reactions of God.

A READER MAY RESPOND: "You argue that there are laws at the heart of life and describe how the world works, but you then to go on to assert that there is no God. Are we to believe that all of life – the infinite expanse of the universe, the burgeoning variety of living things, the beauty and order on every hand – has no meaning, no purpose, no benign end? Are we to believe that we and our world are no more than the product of an endless evolutionary process?"

That is certainly what the available evidence seems to indicate. And it is, in large part, verifiable. Life on earth – and, it would seem, everywhere else – is in constant transition. We ourselves evolved over millions of years from subhuman primates in Africa, and it is not unreasonable to conclude that millions of years from now, some scientist will examine the remains of our civilization and marvel at our primitive ways.

Hell

*I*f there is any single scriptural teaching that negates the concept of a loving God it is the doctrine of eternal punishment in Hell,
a place of torture for all those who refuse to do – or even *fail* to do –
what God wants them to do.

It is a monstrous concept. If a so-called God of love could banish
both the non-believer and the evildoer to a place of endless torment
with no hope for redemption or leniency he would be a sadist beyond
imagining, compared to whom history's most infamous mass-
murderers, Adolf Hitler, Joseph Stalin, and Old Nick himself, would
look like rank amateurs.

The Christian church – while insisting that God is love – has
always made much of the idea that this loving God created and main-
tains a place of eternal punishment where those who reject his only
begotten Son are tormented forever in a lake of fire "where the worm
dieth not and the fire is not quenched."

No appeal. No reprieve. No palliation of their suffering. No hope.

It is unlikely that you will hear it preached on or so much as mentioned in passing in what are sometimes called the "fashionable"
churches, but it is a staple among the Pentecostals and other fundamentalists. Without it, the number of seekers at the mourner's bench
would undoubtedly be fewer.

Many Full Gospel evangelists use the threat of eternal punishment
in the lake of fire as a means to get results. Billy Graham is a firm
believer in an endless Hell and mentions it frequently. Early in the

twentieth century an itinerant Scottish evangelist became renowned in the United States for his ability "to shake sinners over the middle kittles of Hell." It is reported that, when his fulminations against sin and sinners approached their peak, his parishioners used to encourage him by shouting, "Give 'em hell, Reverend! Give 'em hell!"

THE READER MAY BE surprised to learn that the concept of endless torment is not a common theme in the Old Testament. The word Hell is used there mostly to translate the Hebrew word *Sheol*, which means simply "the place of the dead."

In the New Testament the words Hell, Sheol, and Gehenna are used to convey various meanings: the grave, the domain of Satan and his angels, or a place of punishment and retribution for evil deeds. In II Peter 2:4, reference is made to Yahweh casting Satan and his rebellious angels down to Hell where, it would seem, they were not confined but went about among men on earth demonstrating their capacity to make mischief.

Jesus seems to have given some credence to the idea of endless punishment for sin when he told the parable of the rich man, Dives, feasting at his table while the poor man, Lazarus, lay starving at his gate. In the story, the rich man, who showed no compassion for the beggar, dies "and in hell, being in torment, cries out, 'Father Abraham, have mercy on me. Send Lazarus that he may dip the tip of his finger in water and cool my tongue for I am in anguish in this flame.'" Abraham, however, refuses the rich man's plea, informing him that "between us and you there is a great gulf fixed, so that those who would pass from here to you cannot, and none may cross from there to us."

The idea of an endless Hell is a monstrous concept. That a so-called loving Father would condemn his children – no matter how persistently obdurate – to be tortured forever, with no hope for a reprieve, is barbarous beyond belief and can only be dismissed as ancient sadistic nonsense.

Giving Up One's Faith in God

*T*he reader may ask: Why should I abandon my religious beliefs? Why should I say farewell to God? Am I better off believing that there is no God, that life has no essential purpose, that prayer is a pointless exercise, that death is the end?

But none of these is the basic question. The question is not whether one is advantaged by abandoning the Christian faith. It is, rather: *should one continue to base one's life on a system of belief that – for all its occasional wisdom and frequent beauty – is demonstrably untrue?*

In the early seventeenth century nearly everyone in the Western world believed that the sun revolved around the earth. They believed it because the Roman Catholic church said it was so. Moreover, they could confirm it for themselves: Did not the sun rise in the east, traverse the heavens, and set in the west?

And beyond this, the Holy Bible said it was so. Did not God himself cause the sun to stand still in the heavens so that Joshua and the Israelites would have an extended day, thus enabling them to kill every last Amorite? And didn't everyone in Christendom believe it? The Holy Roman Catholic church, the Pope, our rulers, scientists, scholars . . . *everybody?*

Everybody, that is, but one man – an astronomer by the name of Galileo.

Galileo insisted that, although it went contrary to what the Old Testament said, the Roman church taught, and one's eyes could see, the earth revolved around the sun and not the sun around the earth. He was summoned to Rome, warned by the Pope, and told to cease and desist, that his belief contradicted the Holy Bible and the teaching of the church and "was a danger to faith."

But Galileo would not be silenced and, in 1616, he published his conclusions. He was summoned again to Rome, tried by the Inquisition, found guilty, and banished into seclusion – house arrest in an obscure Italian town – for life. Incredibly, it was not until late in the twentieth century – *almost four hundred years later* – that John Paul II conceded publicly that the church had been wrong.

Is it not, in our time, a similar error to continue to believe in and predicate one's life on a concept of God and on a belief system that is outdated and demonstrably untrue?

LET IT BE CLEAR: ceasing to believe in the God one has believed in from childhood is an unsettling experience. It is more comfortable to live by the lessons learned at our mother's knee, to accept the assurances from the church that there is a loving God, that all of life is in his hands, that goodness will triumph over evil, that Jesus Christ will defeat even the last enemy, death, and that "God's in his Heaven" despite manifest evidence that all's *not* "right with the world."

But what if the Bible stories and the theories and teaching of the Christian church about the origin of the world and life on earth aren't true? What if they are no more than primitive history, inscribed by people who believed the world was flat, that there was a personal God, that there was a heaven "up there" and an endless place of suffering "down there"? Should one at this late date in history continue to base one's understanding of life and one's behaviour on an ancient book and a set of inherited beliefs that are outdated and simply untenable in our time?

Beyond that, is it not the height of presumption to assert that, among the multitude of gods in history, *our* God, the God *we* happened to be taught to worship in childhood, is the one and only true God? Is it not a staggering conceit to believe that the religion we chanced to inherit is the only true faith, and that the followers of every other religion in the world are wrong?

WE ARE ALL, IN LARGE part, products of our culture. We speak
the language we speak because it is the language we learned as children and is the language spoken by our family, friends, and country-
men. We eat the kind of food we eat because it is what we were raised
on – we have a taste for it. We most admire men and women who
speak and write in the language we use because we are familiar with
it. And it was almost inevitable that, growing up, we would do as
nearly everyone does, accept "the faith of our fathers."

But having believed from childhood that something is true is anything but a valid reason to continue to believe it as a mature adult. If,
having come of age at the end of the twentieth century, we find our
beliefs no longer credible, should we cling to them simply because
they are a part of our heritage?

This book is not offered as a critique of Christian values or
Christian ideals – they are among the most profound ethical concepts
in history and the author of these lines continues to live by most of
them – but one can accept much of Jesus' teaching without believing
the unbelievable, that this remarkable Palestinian teacher was
Almighty God in the flesh.

THE READER SHOULD be aware that one feels a profound sense of
loss when one abandons any belief system held from childhood.
Those months of indecision during which I struggled with my beliefs
and finally decided to demit the ministry remain the most troubled
and trying of my life.

But it was also a time of new beginnings. The oft-postponed
decision irrevocably made, there came a soaring sense of freedom,
not least, intellectual freedom. It was not that I had felt constrained
in the ministry – other than as the discipline of any commitment
restricts – but there were no longer those subliminal parameters to
put boundaries around my thinking. My mind could freely quest
where it would. I could examine any question without a predis-
position to harmonize it with the body of Christian belief. I felt
loosed. Set free! Some words by the prophet Isaiah express what I
was feeling:

Then the eyes of the blind shall be opened,
and the ears of the deaf unstopped;
then shall the lame man leap like a hart,
and the tongue of the dumb sing for joy.

I was ridding myself of archaic, outdated notions. I was dealing with life as it is. There would be an end to asking the deity for his special intervention on my behalf because I was one of the family. I would stop berating myself for being remiss in following certain prescribed practices, such as praying more, reading the Bible more, fulfilling my religious obligations better. I stopped fretting about sin and began to see selfish behaviour as, essentially, the failure to be caring.

Wrongdoing ceased to be a sin and became, quite simply, doing wrong.

Or, equally important, failing to do right.

There are losses involved when one abandons one's faith, losses such as the pleasant association each Sunday with men and women of like mind, the sense of God's nearness during moments of worship, the feeling of solidarity with one's peers at a Communion service or a Mass. There is a particularly poignant sense of loss at Easter and Christmas. The familiar stories, the sense of wonder, and the warm and wonderful traditions continue to have meaning, but they no longer mean what they did before. And there is the loss of those moments when the familiar phrases of the Bible or the glorious music of Christendom would stimulate a sense of belonging to a community that has endured for thousands of years.

You find yourself rethinking the story of Jesus of Nazareth and, for all its intrinsic fascination, it is not the same. You almost feel that someone you love has died and that you are bereft. And little wonder: no one in Western history has so laid claim to the hearts of men and women as has Jesus of Nazareth. How memorable his brief life. How fascinating his personality. How insightful his teaching. How inspiring his courage. How shattering the horror of his death. How – perhaps more than any other's in Western history – his life has stimulated the potential for goodness in those who take him seriously.

I miss all that, and more. But, analyzed, the feeling is not unlike the occasional yearning to return to one's earlier years when life was simpler. In the end, one must follow the truth as one perceives it. Not to do so is to live a lie.

Growing up isn't easy, but is there any valid option?

Conclusion

Reverence for Life

A man named Albert Schweitzer awoke one morning in his native Alsace and stood at the window of his bedroom on a perfect spring day. He remained there for a while contemplating the beauty before his eyes and thinking of the happiness and satisfactions that life had given him.

He was in the bloom of robust health, had a comfortable living, was a theologian of note, a talented musician, and a world-renowned authority on the organ music of Johann Sebastian Bach, having published, when he was thirty, the classic biography of that musical genius.

His mind turned to another scene. He began to think of the dispossessed of the earth, the poor, the starving, the diseased, the ignorant, those who, while he had everything, had nothing. And in that moment he made the decision that, having received, he must give.

He went on from that morning to study medicine, earned a doctorate at the University of Strasbourg, and then applied to a Christian organization, requesting that he be sent as a medical missionary to the most needy place that could be found. In 1913, at the age of thirty-eight and at the height of his powers, he went to what was then French Equatorial Africa, and established, at Lamberene, a hospital for lepers.

Years later, in 1952, for his work in Africa and in recognition of his many other philosophical, literary, and musical accomplishments, he was awarded the Nobel Peace Prize.

OVER THE YEARS Schweitzer developed a philosophy, a universal concept of ethics which he described in a book called *Reverence for Life*. His essential thesis was that we must respect all life as a manifestation of the divine spirit and that we ought not to destroy any lesser form of life except as is necessary to sustain a higher form. It carried Jesus' injunction, "Love thy neighbour as thyself," into the realm of all living things.

Schweitzer asserted that all life – human, animal, vegetable – is an unmerited gift and must be respected. He argued, for example, that a farmer might legitimately, in the process of growing grain to feed a village, mow down every stalk in an entire wheat field, but walking to his home at the end of the day, that same farmer, a stick in his hand, ought not idly to cut the head from a single stalk of wheat.

I know of no higher or more practical concept as an approach to life. It asserts one's obligation to respect *all* living things, human, animal, and vegetable. Our failure to do this has – on the eve of the twenty-first century – brought us to where life on earth is in increasing jeopardy and we and our world are in danger of self-destruction – not some day in the dim mists of a distant future but, very possibly, within the next two hundred years.

Questions to Ask Yourself

*I*s it not foolish to close one's eyes to the reality that much of the Christian faith is simply impossible to accept as fact? And is it not a fundamental error to base one's life on theological concepts formulated centuries ago by relatively primitive men who believed that the world was flat, that Heaven was "up there" somewhere, and that the universe had been created and was controlled by a jingoistic and intemperate deity who would punish you forever if you did not behave exactly as instructed?

Listed below is a repetition of some of the questions raised in the preceding pages. Put them to yourself.

- Is it not likely that had you been born in Cairo you would be a Muslim and, as 840 million people do, would believe that "there is no God but God and Muhammad is his prophet"?
- If you have been born in Calcutta would you not in all probability be a Hindu and, as 650 million people do, accept the Vedas and the Upanishads as sacred scriptures and hope sometime in the future to dwell in Nirvana?
- Is it not probable that, had you been born in Jerusalem, you would be a Jew and, as some 13 million people do, believe that Yahweh is God and that the Torah is God's Word?
- Is it not likely that had you been born in Peking, you would be one of the millions who accept the teachings of the Buddha or

Confucius or Lao-Tse and strive to follow their teachings and example?

- Is it not likely that you, the reader, are a Christian because your parents were before you?
- If there is a loving God, why does he permit – much less create – earthquakes, droughts, floods, tornadoes, and other natural disasters which kill thousands of innocent men, women, and children every year?
- How can a loving, omnipotent God permit – much less create – encephalitis, cerebral palsy, brain cancer, leprosy, Alzheimer's, and other incurable illnesses to afflict millions of men, women, and children, most of whom are decent people?
- How could a loving Heavenly Father create an endless Hell and, over the centuries, consign millions of people to it because they do not or cannot or will not accept certain religious beliefs? And, having done so, how could he torment them *forever*?
- Why are there literally hundreds of Christian denominations and independent congregations, all of them basing their beliefs on the Bible, and most of them convinced that all the others are, in some ways, wrong?
- If all Christians worship the same God, why can they not put aside their theological differences and co-operate actively with one another?
- If God is a loving Father, why does he so seldom answer his needy children's prayers?
- How can one believe the biblical account of the creation of the world in six days when every eminent physicist agrees that all living species have evolved over millions of years from primitive beginnings?
- Is it possible for an intelligent man or woman to believe that God fashioned the first male human being from a handful of dust and the first woman from one of the man's ribs?
- Is it possible to believe that the Creator of the universe would personally impregnate a Palestinian virgin in order to facilitate getting his Son into the world as a man?
- The Bible says that "the Lord thy God is a jealous God." But if

you are omnipotent, omniscient, omnipresent, eternal, and the creator of all that exists, of whom could you possibly be jealous?

- Why, in a world filled with suffering and starvation, do Christians spend millions on cathedrals and sanctuaries and relatively little on aid to the poor and the needy?
- Why does the omnipotent God, knowing that there are tens of thousands of men, women, and children starving to death in a parched land, simply let them waste away and die when all that is needed is rain?
- Why would the Father of *all* mankind have a Chosen People and favour them over the other nations on earth?
- Why would a God who is "no respecter of persons" prohibit adultery and then bless, honour, and allow to prosper a king who had seven hundred wives and three hundred concubines?
- Why is the largest Christian church controlled entirely by men, with no woman – no matter how pious or gifted – permitted to become a priest, a monsignor, a bishop, an archbishop, a cardinal, or pope?
- Jesus' last words to his followers were "Go ye into all the world and preach the Gospel to every creature. And, lo, I am with you always." But, despite this and to this date – some two thousand years later – billions of men and women have never so much as heard the Christian Gospel. Why?

I Believe

Because I do not want to end on a negative note, permit me to summarize what I *do* believe:

- I believe that there is no supreme being with human attributes – no God in the biblical sense – but that all life is the result of timeless evolutionary forces, having reached its present transient state over millions of years.
- I believe that there is what may best be described as a Life Force, a First Cause, a Primal Energy, a Life Essence, and that it is the genesis of all that is, from the simplest atom to the entirety of the expanding universe.
- I believe that the Life Force is not a "being." It does not love nor can it be loved: it simply is.
- I believe that there is no Father in Heaven who can be persuaded by our prayers, but that meditation in the form of prayer can be an instrument of growth.
- I believe that our world was born in finite time and will, in its time, perish.
- I believe it likely that there are millions of populated worlds in the universe, each at different stages of evolution, some dying, some being born.
- I believe that genus *Homo* is no more than the leading edge of the universal evolutionary process on earth, but that he has more capacity for good *and* evil than any other creature.

- I believe that selfishness is the root of all evil and that caring is the greatest good.
- I believe that we as individuals are in large part predestined by our genetic inheritance but that we are free within these limits to make what we will of our lives.
- I believe that, because we have the ability to control our actions and to discriminate between what we understand to be good or bad, we are responsible for the way we live.
- I believe that, because we are capable of making rational choices, we have the potential to make the world a better place – or to destroy it.
- I believe that the greatest motivating force in life is love. Caring for someone we will be motivated to seek the best for that person and will be ennobled in so doing.
- I believe that you cannot love your neighbour as yourself but that you should care about your neighbour, whoever he is and wherever he lives, help him when you can and co-operate with him to make our world a better place.
- I believe that life yields rewards and punishments but that we cannot expect and will not receive any special favours from any alien source.
- I believe that, in common with all living creatures, we die and cease to exist as an entity.
- I believe that life is the superlative gift and is to be celebrated.